MAN'S WAY

WALTER GOLDSCHMIDT
University of California

Man's Way A PREFACE TO

THE UNDERSTANDING

OF HUMAN SOCIETY

A HOLT-DRYDEN BOOK

HOLT, RINEHART AND WINSTON, INC.
NEW YORK

23195-0119

Library of Congress Catalog Card Number: 59-5926

June, 1962

To my teachers:
George C. Engerrand and Clarence E. Ayers
of the University of Texas,
Alfred L. Kroeber, Paul S. Taylor,
and the late Robert H. Lowie
of the University of California, Berkeley,
and to those sterner taskmasters,
my students

Contents

Contents

Contents

MAN'S WAY

Introduction

MAN'S WAY examines both the manner in which men live and the route that man has traversed through time. The dual meaning of the title is intentional, illustrating in a single phrase the central theme of this book. In order to understand man's cultural development, one must also understand the way he lives, and in order to understand his ways, one must know the road he has traveled.

Man's way, in the first sense, is to live in a society of fellow men, according to established custom. Man's commitment to social existence has consequences, and in this book we set forth the general features of all societies. While custom—culture, in modern anthropological parlance—sets down the details of proper social behavior in any one time and place, custom is itself shaped by these requirements of social life.

Man's way, in the second sense, has been an evolutionary development involving the greater and greater mastery of the physical world. This has enabled him not only to spread into all quarters of the globe, but also to increase in numbers and to live in ever larger aggregates. This, in turn, has created new and different problems in the organization of society, and has required different ways of living.

The character and evolution of social forms is our concern, but man himself is at the center of our interests. To have a proper view of society requires a proper concept of the human animal. Therefore we boldly put forth our assumption that man is by nature committed to social existence, and is therefore inevitably involved in the dilemma between serving his own interests and recognizing those of the group to which he belongs. Insofar as this dilemma can be resolved, it is resolved by the fact that man's self-interest can best be served through his commitment to his fellows.

Man's way is a hard one, a faltering one. It is hard because the commitment to social existence and the dependence upon accumulated culture place limitations upon the free operation of self-interest; it is faltering because the manifestations of self-interest within the cultural milieu have not always served the ends of continued survival or continuous growth. But through time and with many false moves and casualties, man has gained an increasing mastery of his world. And with each successive step forward on the technological level, new problems have required new solutions, some technical but many social. In meeting these social problems, man has founded a wide variety of cultural forms, of which many have been recurrent because they are the obvious solutions to the demands placed upon social existence.

Modern society is a product of this evolution, a process that continues to operate with all its force. We are witness to the emergence of a new kind of society, made both possible and necessary by the magnificent development of our technical competence, which has given time and space new meanings and which, too, has created such destructive powers that warfare is no longer a luxury that the species can afford. These developments make it necessary for us to evolve the institutions requisite for social life in this new world. Since social evolution (unlike biological) can proceed through man's own conscious efforts, an understanding of the nature of human society can be useful to the survival of mankind.

In this book we are concerned with the understanding itself; not with problems of amelioration; not with programs of action. It is one of the universal features of social systems that man provides himself with a mode of explaining the events around him. The modern cosmology is scientific, and the understanding of man and his social environment must fit this system of scientific understanding. We sometimes feel that the modern scholar, interested in contributing to the understanding of some segment of the universe, is the direct descendant of those priests along the ancient Nile, whose astronomical observations were concerned first and foremost with a comprehension of the world, but whose accumulated understanding (however faulty) made possible the prediction of the seasons of inundation of that life-giving river. Thus their understanding contributed to the welfare of their society. So, too, with the modern sciences. So too, perhaps, the scientific understanding of man's way.

The Biological Constant

ANIMAL ENDS AND CULTURAL MEANS

MAN IS AN ANIMAL and was an animal before he became cultured. It is in general correct to speak of man's animal characteristics as being laid down before the development of his culture, and as being a condition of man to which his culture had to adjust. As an animal, man is endowed with certain qualities which make culture both possible and practical. By whatever evolutionary process he came by it, man has the characteristic of standing on his hind legs, thus freeing his forelimbs from the function of locomotion. These forelimbs in turn have developed into remarkable instruments, with a ball-and-socket joint at the shoulder, an elbow joint, a rotating joint at the wrist, and a set of five digits (all but one triply jointed) all combined to make it possible for man to lift and handle heavy objects and still to make very delicate and refined grasping adjustment. This built-in tool has made all other tools possible. Associated with these special characteristics is man's stereoscopic vision, which allows for the precise judgments of distance that are a great help in making tools and such other functions as shooting and jumping. Man's capacity to make things with his hands has, in fact, given him the tools with which he has conquered every part of the world: this aspect of his physical endowment is crucial to the survival of culture. Physical anthropologists and medical men have concerned themselves with the disadvantages of upright posture and the internal dislocations it has caused; but none go so far as to forget the debt which human ingenuity owes to those presumably arboreal ancestors who first underwent this biological alteration.

This whole matter seems so self-evident that it need not be spelled out in further detail. It does seem worth while, however, to emphasize the point that this tool-making capacity is a necessary element in the development of culture, that it has given man his evolutionary survival value and his world dominance.

Man is not the only animal who makes things. The bee-hive, the bird's nest, the beaver dam, and innumerable other structures in nature are products of animal manufacture. The difference is that man *learns* how to make things; unlike the bees he does not inherit the knowledge of how to do so. The implications of this difference are far-reaching. Not least important is the fact that since man has learned to make things, he can learn to make them better or differently, or he can even forget how to make them. The learned ability, therefore, has in itself a certain flexibility which gives man's behavior a new level of operation. This level is the cultural, the level of learning to do things according to customary procedures.

Man is also not the only animal that learns things. Conditioning has been shown to operate on such low biological levels as that of the angleworm, which can learn to make the proper turning in a T-maze. With respect to learning, the difference between man and his fellow creatures is a difference in degree, but that degree is very extensive. It is not unlikely that with the growth in the use of learned behavior, man has actually undergone some attrition in his instinctive reactions. At any rate, all anthropologists and biologists agree that whatever remains of the instinctive in human behavior, its function is far less important in life activities than is the function of learning and learned behavior. For that matter, it is seldom useful to speak of instincts in man. Although he does have instinctual elements in his behavior, so far as we know they are of a more generalized kind, and perhaps better called needs or drives.

Man's dependence upon learning has another facet connected with his own unique endowment: speech. Man is the only animal that has language, though he is not the only animal that communicates nor even the only one that communicates by sound. The dog's bark and growl, the calls of birds, frogs' croaking, for example, are definite communications. They announce the proximity of danger or the desire and readiness to mate; they communicate immediate and pressing conditions. Language does this—but it does more. It is not merely a more complicated form of animal communication; it is a form which enables persons to relate matters in time and place and with respect to one another. With language it is possible to discuss matters of the past or the future, to discuss events and places which are distant, which do not exist, or which cannot exist. A person gifted in the use of language can create a kind of reality which may become more real to his listeners than the actual physical world. This capacity is universal among men and is limited to mankind. No other animal has been discovered with such a system of communication—with the partial exception of the honeybee, which apparently communicates the distance and direction of food by means of body gestures. Man's nearest relatives, the apes, have been subjected to intensive linguistic training, but always without result. The implications are obvious and far-reaching.

Though we do not know when language developed, we

know that it is universal among men, and we presume it
to be as old as any other part of human culture. Indeed,
we take this ability to communicate as being a precondition
to human society, and it is impossible to conceive of culture without it. Since man's peculiar technical capacities
are transmitted by learning, language is necessary to the
transmission of the detailed knowledge that constitutes
the cultural mode of behavior. We do not know just what
in the physiological sense provides man's capacity for
language. Presumably, certain areas of the brain were
developed which gave him this power. But whatever evolu-
tional process was involved, it is useful to realize that this
capacity for language is a capacity not only to respond to
symbols but to create them—for *language is symbolic
behavior*. The words on this page are symbolic representations of vocalizations, and these in turn evoke in the mind
of the reader certain images and feelings that are more or
less the counterpart of what was intended. Man has the
unique capacity of creating innumerable symbols.

It has been suggested that the symbol is the basic unit
of culture in the sense that the cell is the unit of living
matter. Perhaps this is no more than a figure of speech, but
it is a useful one. However real the actual world may be,
the cultural world is learned largely through speech. Since
it has been filtered through the symbol system of language,
the cultural world that man perceives is a symbolic one.
We cannot appreciate the character of human life without
taking cognizance of this need to symbolize. The problem
of symbols will beset us throughout our discussion of social
life, for human social systems revolve about the symbols
which man has created and to which, in turn, he responds
—often with passionate intensity.

The features mentioned thus far—man's tool-making
capacity, his emphasis on learned behavior, his language
—are distinctive in man and set him apart from other

animals. But some features of the human heritage are not distinctive; they are common to all living things and yet have important effects on man's social behavior and on the characteristics of culture. Fundamental among these are the basic drives: hunger, thirst, sexual gratification and procreation, and the seeking of physical comfort. All these and other things man shares with other animals, yet culture is inevitably shaped in terms of these drives and every social system must take cognizance of them. This is not to say that the drives must universally be met—that people cannot go hungry for a time or forgo sexual gratification— but rather that the drives exist and that if they are not to be met, the necessary social institutions must be provided either to give psychological support to the restraint of appetites or to engender physical force to prevent the satisfaction of them.

There is a further point here. Although these drives may be thought of as animal drives, everywhere in human societies they are given cultural interpretation. Man as an animal must eat, but man as a cultured animal must eat certain things and avoid others; he must eat at certain times and in certain ways, and according to certain carefully prescribed customs. Man must mate. But the cultured animal must select his mate according to certain rules, and the act of procreation is circumscribed by a welter of culturally established demands. We might put the matter this way: that even man's most basic animal drives are given a symbolic content and their fulfillment is caught up in the symbol system that is the culture of that particular people. For this reason it is never possible to see man operating as a mere animal; he is always and forever a cultured animal, even in the fulfillment of his most elementary biological needs.

It is worth while to note that these biological needs can in fact not only be restrained but completely suppressed by the action of culture. People in all parts of the world (though not necessarily in every culture) will accept death before they will suffer dishonor—as their particular culture defines dishonor. Men will starve rather than violate culturally established restrictions on biologically satisfactory food. Men will cease to procreate and to satisfy their sexual urges in response to religious convictions with respect to chastity and sin. There is no more impressive indication of the power of symbols as determinative of human action than this recurrent cultural phenomenon.

PROLONGED MATURATION AND CULTURE

We have already touched upon the fact that man's behavior is overwhelmingly learned behavior, that he acts in response to conditioning rather than to biologically inherited patterns of activity. Man shares with all other mammals and many other forms of life the fundamental fact that he comes into being helpless and dependent and must be nurtured over a period of time. The length of this time is longer for man than for any other animal on record; even the largest, the whale, becomes mature in something like half the time that it takes human beings to mature. This protracted period of dependence has three basic consequences: (1) it makes requisite the universal existence of institutions designed for the care and feeding of the immature and helpless; (2) it forces upon the growing infant an acquiescence to the demands of pre-existing, established social and cultural systems; and (3) it provides an environment in which the learning that is so important to the cultured animal can take place.

The first of these three consequences of prolonged human immaturity is the universal existence of what we may here call the *family*. The family, consisting of a marital pair (or group) of adults together with their immature offspring, is a practically universal aspect of human social systems. Though human cultures have played out all the possible permutations, variations, and embellishments on the family as an institution, a basic unity underlies all human societies, from the simplest to the most complex. The rare and often temporary exceptions are significant only at the believe-it-or-not level of discourse.

Closely associated with this phenomenon is the general notion of kinship. In all societies each person normally is a participant in two family institutions: that into which he is born and in which he establishes relationships with his parents and siblings; and that which he creates upon marriage, in which he establishes relationships with his spouse and children. Since each of these persons with whom he has such established ties in turn has other established ties, every individual in every society—whatever else may be true about its organization—finds himself in a network of kin relationships which have permanent and enduring implications for his patterns of social interaction.

Another human physiological characteristic may contribute to the universal institution of the family. This is the fact that man, unlike most other mammals, is in permanent sexual readiness throughout his mature years. Thus there is a direct sexual bond between male and female that is continuously reinforced. This sets him in contrast to those animals which have rutting seasons and therefore no sexual inducement to permanent and continuous ties. Needless to say, this has nothing to do with the permanence of a particular marriage, nor with affection or love between individuals, but merely refers to the sexual relationship between men and women.

The prolonged maturation period of the human animal has implications for the learning of culture. All people enter their culture and their society by way of the womb.

They take their position in that society and acquire its culture in the process of growing up. In other words, they accept the implications of the particular symbol system of their culture and the pattern of organization of their society while they are still helpless to reject it. By the time they have achieved the maturity which might enable them to act independently of the cultural dictates, they are already imbued with and caught in its assumptions and imperatives. It is this aspect of cultural transmission which gives it continuity. This is demonstrated by the fact that those parts of culture which are laid down earliest and lie deepest in the unconscious attitudes are always the most difficult to change with changing circumstances or (as in the case of modern migrations) changing cultures.

Here we must return to the matter of language, for it is important to realize that much of culture is acquired through verbal learning before it is acquired through experience. The world of reality for man is a cultural world, and a cultural world is in large measure a verbal one. The classifications that are implicit in every language, the values that are implicit in word choice, the definitions of the situation as they are expressed in ordinary discourse and in tales and narratives, all tend to set for the members of that culture the "true" character of their world. Few indeed are the human experiences which have not been received verbally before they are experienced in actuality.

There is one other feature of man's make-up that calls forth a certain amount of speculation. Man is a mammal, which means primarily that the female gives birth to living young and suckles them during infancy. All mammals, and not a few other animals, must therefore have the capacity to restrain their desires for personal satisfaction in the form of food, drink, the seeking of comfort, or the flight from danger, in order to bear, nurse, and protect their offspring. The chemistry that underlies these patterns of activity is obscure, but the reality of such activities is attested on all sides. It seems to me that we must recognize that some physiological quality is operative in these forms of life which make them forgo their immediate individual satisfactions for the sake of some ultimate group survival. Whether we speak of this as conscience is perhaps a matter of philosophy, but there can be no doubt that it manifests itself as the internalization of a responsibility that has a moral consequence. Man also recognizes external demands that place limits on his free pursuit of self-interest and usually conforms to them. In all societies man recognizes a public interest—in the fashion his culture has set forth—to which he regularly (but not universally) conforms.

Such speculations lead to the consideration of subjects which in religious discourse are referred to as the inherent goodness of man, original sin, and the conflict between good and evil. Here, however, it is best to divest them of moralistic implications and consider merely a reasonable set of assumptions out of which a coherent analysis of social behavior can be developed. It seems fair enough to assume that everywhere man is caught between the conflicting interests of his own personal ends and aims and a recognition of the proper and legitimate interest of his fellow men. He is by nature drawn to living in social aggregates and must therefore have the capacity to suppress his personal desires when these are in conflict with the expectations of his society. Yet he must and does see these external, communal obligations also in terms of a prevailing self-interest. It is not an enlightened one, but rather one that has been inculcated as part of his cultural training. Much in culture involves the delicate balance between these opposing forces: personal versus group interest.

THE NEED FOR POSITIVE AFFECT

Most anthropolgists would accept the preceding discussion with little question or change of emphasis, but one additional element in the character of the human animal must be put forth. It is a postulate, at present unproved and perhaps not susceptible to proof, but it is one that seems necessary if we are to arrive at a satisfactory understanding of human society. This additional element is a drive, perhaps unique to man, which can be called (for want of a better phrase) the *need for positive affect*.

Need for positive affect means that each person craves response from his human environment. It may be viewed as a hunger, not unlike that for food, but more generalized. Under varying conditions it may be expressed as a desire for contact, for recognition and acceptance, for approval, for esteem, or for mastery.

Desire for positive affect should be seen as separate from but not unrelated to the desire for sexual gratification; it should not be considered one with the erotic, though in its manifestation in society it is often confused with it. The ultimate source of this need is viewed as biological rather than cultural. This is not to suggest that there is a particular gene or specific physiologic locus for such an element, but rather that there is in man's make-up a constellation of conditions which result in this general characteristic. What these might be I do not venture to state. It is no more mysterious than the inherent tendencies of many species of animals (not always mammals or even vertebrates) to live in close mutual association, and perhaps it is biologically related to these herding orientations. Its manifestations are sufficiently distinct in man, however, to suggest a separate formulation. Those who would avoid all physiological forces in setting the course of human behavior would find the source of this element in man's long physical dependence upon parental care and his consequent conditioning to interrelationships with others. But among other mammals such dependence does not regularly result in permanent group associations, and those animal societies that exist do not have the same characteristics as do societies among human beings. At any rate, these facts alter the case very little. The point is to recognize clearly that this need is not a product of cultural conditioning but underlies it.

This last point is crucial to the entire thesis. Our concern is to explain the general character of social life in all its manifestations as observed by anthropologists and sociologists. The explanation put forth here rests on the assumption that each individual enters into his social relations armed (or burdened, if you wish) with the need for positive affect. Whether he acquires it at the moment of conception, within the womb, or in those early moments of life before he has culture, is a matter of less concern. But without the assumption of the existence of this need, of its universality and its independence of culture, our thesis fails.

The point is elaborated not only because of its importance but also because many anthropologists and most sociologists seem to reject such a postulate. It is more congenial to psychology, especially to Freudian and post-Freudian clinical psychology. In fact, with varying emphasis upon particular manifestations, and in varying degrees of explicitness, it underlies much psychological thinking.

Note was taken above that the postulate is not proved and is unlikely of proof. Research into the animal nature of man unaffected by culture is virtually impossible. The closest effort at such research was made by René A. Spitz in a famous comparative study of two nursery homes: one where the infants were cared for with the typical parental type of handling and the other where, though all physical needs were met, the babies were given no personal interest. In the latter, mortality rate and poor health had the higher incidence. Recent studies of macaque monkeys are suggestive—though we must not forget that these primates are not human beings. Macaque infants were reared with surrogate mothers of two kinds: one a wire scaffolding holding a bottle, the other a similar construction covered with foam rubber and terry cloth and given a face. Even those infants nursed by the wire mother sought comfort and "response" from the more lifelike representation. Thus the postulated need for positive affect is supported by research, yet it is too far-reaching a matter to stand on this and similar studies, with all the methodological difficulties they entail. The need must continue to be viewed as a postulate. If we see it as biological, it is not so much because of its universality as because our theoretical orientation requires a pre-established motive for human acquiescence to the demands of social existence. If we treat it as a product of culture and then explain cultural phenomena in terms of it, we are engaging in circular reasoning. To say it is biological is not to say it is *instinctive*, as that word is habitually used, but rather that it is a generalized behavioral attribute universal to normal human beings that derives directly from some one biological quality (or combination of biological qualities) with which they are endowed. Whatever the source, this need for positive affect is a constant and recurrent element in human social behavior.

As we examine human behavior, we find that persons not only universally live in social systems, which is to say they are drawn together, but also universally act in such ways as to attain the approval of their fellow men. In this search for approval, they willingly and often eagerly undergo physical torture, mental harassment, or death—and even hard work!

Earlier in this chapter, man's physical needs for food and drink and sexual gratification were mentioned. These are personal needs. The need for responsive relationships, however, may be viewed as a social need. An understanding of the dynamic elements in social existence must take cognizance of the inherent conflict between these two needs: the personal and group. Demand for positive affect involves their interrelationship, for it offers the satisfaction of personal ends through, and only through, recognition of societal demands.

Perhaps it is worth while to illustrate this with an analogy. The demand for sexual gratification is a personal need; the desire to engage in the sex act is a physiologic compulsion toward the release of inner tension, however much it may be also caught up in the social system of the culture. But this gratification can best be achieved through a relationship with the sexual partner which is basically social: i.e., the gratification received is proportionate to the gratification given. In this sense, though personal desires and societal demands may be in actual and active conflict, it is still true that the fulfillment of the former can be had only through submission to the latter. This is true if we accept the postulate that man has an established desire for positive affect.

Culture as a learned pattern of actions, beliefs, and feelings shared by a community, and society as a system of interactions and organized relations among its members, have their base in the animal attributes of man. But these animal attributes merely lay down the broad conditions under which culture and society operate. They are not the determinants of cultural forms nor the delineators of social organization. The study of human behavior is no mere adjunct to the physiological sciences. Rather, social phenomena are to be understood in sociological terms, and the central considerations which explain the nature and variety of social forms must rest upon social and cultural dynamics. The biologist recognizes the limitations of biology in the chemical attributes of matter but does not explain the variety of life forms by appealing to the laws of chemistry; so, too, the student of human behavior takes cognizance of the biological constant in assessing the general characteristics of all human social systems, but he does not resort to biological divergencies to explain the variant manifestations of social behavior. The tendency to explain higher-order systems in terms of lower-order phenomena has been called the *reductionist fallacy*. Such a reductionism must be avoided. But it is not reductionism to recognize the raw materials of which the higher-order phenomena are constituted. The biological constant underlies all social systems, but it does not explain those systems or the variations among them.

The Dimensions
of Anthropological Theory

GENERAL CONSIDERATIONS

T HE ULTIMATE TASK of the anthropological enterprise
is to explain the uniformities and diversities in the
natural condition of mankind. Faced with the accumulated
information about human behavior, beliefs, attitudes, economic pursuits, modes of transportation—the whole cab-
bages and kings of cultural phenomena—the anthropologist
attempts to make concatenated sense out of the whole.
Theories endeavoring to explain human behavior can be
traced back to the ancient Greeks (e.g. Herodotus) and
even further back to the cosmological and cosmogenic assumptions of primitive peoples prior to the invention of
writing. But anthropology as a discipline, that is, the regular and orderly examination of the data on human behavior, did not emerge until the middle of the nineteenth
century. By then, the general value of science was recognized and the scientific examination of all aspects of nature
was being undertaken. With the acceptance of man as a
part of nature, it was inevitable that the study of man
should be included in this broad scientific cosmology. This
chapter offers an examination, not of the history of anthro-

pological thought, but of the different orientations which anthropological explanations of human behavior have taken.

The theological may be eliminated from among these at the outset. It is obvious that the thesis underlying this volume, as of most anthropological thought, is that man as an animal is a part of nature and a product of biological evolution and is subject to the natural forces and systems of causation applicable to all natural phenomena. Human divergences are not the creation of a deity; they are not to be seen as deriving from the sons of Shem and the sons of Ham.

Short shrift may also be given to the physiological explanations. The biological considerations in the preceding chapter refer to conditions respecting all mankind, but the differences between peoples are not seen as the result of divergent physiological manifestations. To explain them thus would be to assume that culture varies with physiology, that man's variant cultural behaviors are a product of variant physical heredities. Such a position would be denied by all modern anthropologists with few and unimportant exceptions. The world has offered a good laboratory in which to demonstrate that changes in culture and in economic circumstances do not rest on physiological differences. The quick changes in culture, the ready adaptation of alien cultures to new ones under favorable circumstances, the adjustment of primitive peoples to the modern world, and the technical advances which have been made by many American Indians, all testify to the fact that cultural differences do not represent physiological differences. The differences between the least advanced primitive community and the most elevated and imperial cultural system is not a difference in genes; it is not a difference in IQ; it is not a difference that has any kind of physical explanation.

Social and cultural differences must be explained in social and cultural terms.

We may also eliminate from our consideration a disappearing minority, the environmental determinists. Like physiology, environment is external to the social situation. Every culture is affected by the physical environment in which it operates, and the geographical factor will enter into our understanding of the factors which determine cultural forms. But culture is no mere reflection of environment; it is a creative thing which can within limits alter the environment. Significantly, neither the theological, physiological, nor environmentalist explanation has ever had a large part in anthropological theories about the human condition.

Let us consider the major orientations that have actually dominated anthropological thought for the past century. Though we shall not be unmindful of the history of our discipline, we are now more concerned with points of view than with temporal sequence.

CLASSIC EVOLUTIONISM

Anthropology began to develop a consistent and respectable theory in the latter half of the nineteenth century, the scientific period of the naturalists. Two sister sciences, biology and geology, made great strides in their careful examination of the natural world. Naturalists had gone to all parts of the earth and had described the plants and the animals of the world in minute and careful detail. The classification of plants and animals initiated by the Swedish naturalist Linnaeus gave recognition to the relationship between life forms and thus was a fundamental step in the development of evolutionary understanding, though not always appreciated as such. The concept of evolution received explicit formulation in Charles Darwin's *The Origin of Species*, published in 1859. The essential validity of the Darwinian hypothesis in evolutionary development offered scientists a broad concept under which they could unify the various phenomena of living matter. It became clear that man was a part of this system.

At the same time, the science of geology was making grave inroads into the theological concept of the origin of the earth. Careful examination of the stratified rocks and of fossil remains in them supported a notion of the gradual evolution of the earth, and of life itself.

Meanwhile, an obscure man in France had been examining other fossil remains. The thunderstones of the European peasant, certain round, conical, or tapering stones, formerly thought to be thunderbolts and regarded with much awe, were given new meaning by an amateur French scientist who claimed that they were the products of antediluvian man. De Perthes' views were scorned in favor of Biblical understanding of human origins. But when a number of British scientists, including the great geologist, Sir Charles Lyell, examined the data and declared the conclusions of de Perthes to be sound, these discoveries had the effect of bringing mankind quite closely into the system of geological-biological evolutionary explanations. With Lyell's seal of approval, analysis of archeological sequence was quickly developed, and man's place in nature was clarified for the scholars of the day. For clearly man's techniques showed that same progressive development that characterized animal evolution. The contemporary success of evolutionary theory in biology and the obvious analogy suggested by these primitive artifacts virtually forced an evolutionary conception on anthropology.

One might presume that this evolutionary hypothesis would have rested on biological assumptions, that the divergent varieties of human beings and human cultures would be seen as products of different levels of biological development, that the evolution of culture and society was an external manifestation of inherently biological change. Such theories with racist tones had some popular appeal, but very little influence on anthropological thought. Rather, evolutionary theory in anthropology was evolutionary by analogy. The assumption was not that men stood at different biological or physiological levels, but rather that man was one, and that what evolved was culture, presumably by an inner dynamic of its own. Evolutionary theory in anthropology is, and has always been, culture theory and not biological theory.

Both early biological and social evolution had certain doctrinaire elements that must be examined. These elements were closely associated with the philosophical mood of the time, laid down in part by current religious theory concerning the origin and character of man and in part by the great social and economic expansion of Europe during the nineteenth century. European man saw progress all around him, saw growth, development, perfectibility, and, above all, man's mastery of his own destiny. The evolutionary doctrine therefore tended repeatedly to contain qualities of inevitability, teleology, and ethnocentrism. Evolution was generally regarded as the unfolding of an inevitable course of events, so that any primitive society, left long enough to itself, would inevitably develop the character and institutions of the most advanced form, just as biological evolution assumed (erroneously) that such would be the case with respect to the lower orders of life. Evolution was regarded as having an inner dynamic, as being an almost spiritual force in the unfolding of the protoplasmic destiny; in a sense, the Shakespearean sonnet was thought to have been foreordained in the primordial ooze. Finally modern life, particularly middle-class Victorian life, was regarded as the end product of this evolutionary sequence. In evolutionary theory, man was the masterpiece of Nature's handiwork, and Western civilization was the masterpiece of social evolution.

The evolutionary explanation of social forms required a taxonomy not unlike that of the Linnaean classification in botany; and the assumption that different orders of society could be arranged hierarchically in terms of increased evolutionary development, just as reptiles precede mammals, amphibians precede reptiles, and fishes precede amphibians. Innumerable efforts were made to formulate such classifications; but most of them reduced themselves to a three-class system, subdivided in a variety of ways.

The clearest exponent of this three-stage evolutionary system was the American, Lewis Henry Morgan, who named his three stages: *savagery, barbarism,* and *civilization.* Roughly speaking, Morgan's savages were those peoples who lived off natural products without replenishing them by agriculture or animal husbandry. (Today we generally call them hunters and food-gatherers.) His barbarians were those peoples who had primitive forms of agricultural techniques, who lived without the use of metal, and who had no writing. (In current terminology, they are usually called horticultural and herding peoples.) Civilization began with the combination of writing, metal, and statecraft. These distinctions remain of basic importance, and will play a considerable part in the theory that follows.

The evolutionary position, however, not only held that these were sequential in time, but that such a sequence was repetitive and inevitable. Contemporary savages were seen as representing an earlier stage through which all barbarians and civilized peoples had passed; they represented a precondition in the same sense that the shark represented an earlier condition in biological evolution toward mammals. Implicit in this theory was the notion that these developments into barbaric and civilized forms had occurred repeatedly and, if the natural world of society were left alone, would continue to recur wherever people remained in this backward state.

Evolutionary theory did not merely categorize human social systems in a sequence of presumed temporal development. More importantly, it provided a framework for the development of institutions and their manifestations as they emerged from the primordial condition of man. Marriage, for instance, was an institution subjected to elaborate evolutionary analysis. In such analyses, the ethnocentric patterns of belief set the direction of evolution. Monogamy was viewed as the highest form of relationship between the sexes; hence divergences from monogamy were considered earlier stages in the evolution of the marriage contract. Before monogamy came polygamy; before polygamy were the group marriages (a number of men and a number of women in direct and continuing sexual relationship), a pattern of marriage that has been reported in a few instances. Under these assumptions, the logical opposite of permanent and enduring monogamous relationships is a state of promiscuity. Both the oppositeness and the analogy to "lower orders of animals" implicit in such a condition suggest it as the primitive kind of mating.

Parenthetically, the efforts to demonstrate the earlier existence of such a system has resulted in the development of the most consistently important aspect of the study of human society. Morgan believed that patterns of kin relationships, such as that of aboriginal Hawaii, where a person referred to all women of his mother's generation as "mother" and all men of his father's generation as "father," was a kind of atavistic remnant of earlier patterns of procreation in which a person did not know who his uterine mother or his actual father were. It was atavistic in the sense that the wisdom tooth is presumed to be a remnant of a period when the human jaw was larger and stronger. Such a view, of course, is no longer tenable, but Morgan's efforts to substantiate this theory of the evolution of family life brought forth the study of the variety of kinship behavior, which remains a dominant subject of anthropological inquiry today.

The meaning and implications of systems of kinship behavior for patterning interpersonal relations among men will be discussed later; the above example merely demonstrates the kind of conclusions sought and theories developed under the major theoretical tenets of evolutionism. Similar evolutionary sequences were projected for religion (belief in spirits, animism, polytheism, monotheism), for law, for property, and the like. These efforts have not been so rewarding in further anthropological inquiry.

Early evolutionary theory frequently lacked rigorous methodology and often was based on extremely sparse data and tenuous assumptions. Particular forms of evolutionism became highly theoretical and remote from the reality which they were endeavoring to explain, and they left out any systematic explanation of large sectors of human behavior. Meanwhile, Western man had lost some of his sense of certainty that he was the inevitable end product of a divine evolutionary providence, and evolutionary theory waned with the closing of the nineteenth century. But, however moribund it became and however frequently it was officially pronounced dead, it has survived to the present and remains a force in the explanatory system of modern social anthropology.

HISTORICAL EXPLANATIONS

In the twentieth century, evolutionary theory no longer satisfied the intellectual quest for an explanation of man's variant behavior. In fact, a reaction developed against any kind of theoretical construct and, in America at least, the dominant motifs of this reaction were empiricism and an emphasis on the unique historical event. The first was partly a response to awakened scientism and the growing need to make a closer and more detailed examination of the world of primitive man. It was also a quite conscious response to the recognition that the raw data of anthropology were disappearing as native peoples became extinct or were engulfed by Western civilization.

The most forceful attack on the evolutionary schemata came from America, spearheaded by Franz Boas, who was a proponent of the historical viewpoint. Boas was a trained geographer from Germany who had early engaged in research among the Eskimo. His background was scholarly, cautious, and, unlike that of most existing theorists, his ideas were based upon firsthand experience with foreign and primitive cultures. His mind was not simple nor his writings monolithic, but his general effect—and he directly or indirectly trained the bulk of two generations of scholars—was the concentration on the particular and the assumption that behavior was the product of a singular history and not the result of any general scheme. His attitude has been viewed as antitheoretical. It was, rather, historical. In his outlook, the Arunta or the Andamanese* were not as they were because they were caught on the rungs of an evolutionary ladder, but because of the circumstances of their own particular history.

Today such historical orientation appears to be a kind of nihilist theory: the notion that no general principles can be seen in the social systems of the world but that each is the chance result of a unique history. In this view, the anthropologist who would "explain" the cultural behavior

---

* The geographical location of these and other peoples mentioned throughout the book may be found under their index entries.

of any people whose life he was studying—the Pueblo Indians, say—would view their culture as the end product
of their own history, starting with the culture which they
brought to the area and which was influenced by their own
successive inventions and the borrowings from their neighbors. Anthropology, it was said, had the choice between
becoming history or nothing. And culture, it was said, was
a thing of shreds and patches. Robert H. Lowie, Boas's early
student who made this statement, did, to be sure, disavow
the intent, but the phrase has hung on as an expression
of historic theory, not so much because Lowie believed it
as because it was implicit in the theoretical writings of
historic-minded American anthropologists.

If culture is viewed as the result of unique and fortuitous
historic events, then the obvious job of anthropologists is
to uncover the diverse threads of history that have led to
the diverse cultures in the world. One primary method
was by means of archeology, a fact which may suggest why
archeology in America is a branch of anthropology, while
in Europe it tends to be a separate discipline. Another
means was through careful examination of the legends of
the people. But conclusions drawn from legends are always
suspect, for legends are notorious for their coloration of
events. The third was to try to uncover the particular history of each particular element that made up the culture,
each custom, each technique, each trait. To do this, it
would be necessary to find out just where each element in
culture was to be found and to give a detailed analysis of
these customs and culture traits. A principle developed in
biology, that a species or stock which had a wide dispersion
over the earth was older than a related one which had a
narrower distribution, was adapted to the uses of such
history.

Let us examine the background of thinking here. Mankind was viewed as everywhere equal in capacity, generally

governed by custom and tradition, and little given to innovation, though capable of developing new techniques. He was not rational in the sense that necessity was the mother of invention, that culture was a response to need, or that he was primarily motivated by economic forces. The study of culture was the study of the customs which governed such people. Customs originated in various parts of the world, more by accident than design. Often they were invented more than once. A great deal of American Indian culture involved knowledge that could hardly have been transmitted across the ocean, either because it was unique to America (as, for example, the use of rubber), because it involved specific differences (as the cultivation of maize), or because of the timing and distance involved (as with the development of writing or the concept of the zero). But if an item could be found in more or less continuous distribution over a part of the earth, or if it was so complex and arbitrary as to make a separate development seem highly improbable, then it was presumed to have had a single origin and to have spread (by diffusion, as the academic phrase had it) from some single source.

Thus it was that the anthropologist's task was to find the distribution and variants of each separate culture element: bear ceremonialism in circumpolar areas, the sun dance on the American plains, moccasins and snowshoes, gambling games, the trickster motif in folktale and mythology, and so on and so forth. By careful analysis of variants, by some considerations of practicality and location, by connecting one item with another, it was possible to construct the history of one particular trait as it spread in prehistoric times, and sometimes to set up a reasonable hypothesis for the locus of its origin. Then, presumably, it would be possible to piece together the history of a particular people from the history of its separate major elements. Indeed much progress was made along these lines and is still being

made. The historic spread of the Athapascan-speaking Indians from interior Alaska to California and to the American Southwest, the diffusion of Negro elements into the
American South, the original peopling of Polynesia, have
been more or less satisfactorily reconstructed. The detailed
methods by which such historical reconstruction could be
made were set out by Edward Sapir. The American anthropologist, Clark Wissler, applied this technique most assidu-
ously, and in doing so succeeded in demonstrating its
fundamental weakness.

In his *The Relation of Nature to Man in Aboriginal
America,* Wissler plotted the occurrence of divergent forms
of various aspects of culture. He endeavored to show that
there was a tendency for the variants to be distributed in
concentric rings, with the simplest in the peripheral ring
and the most elaborated or most developed form in the
center ring. He applies these techniques both to highly
specialized elements, such as variants on a religious cere-
mony, and to broad conceptual ones, such as the distinctions between hunters, agriculturists, and empires. Wissler
argues that the development is from the simple to the
complex, and that such distribution shows not only the
course of events, but the centers of origin, for he believes
that the centers had the base traits earlier and built upon
these innovations which did not spread so widely. Many
of these distributions involved the Indians of the Plains,
where we know from subsequent data that there was much
physical movement of people and change in culture between Coronado and Lewis and Clark as a result of the
introduction of the horse and other direct and indirect
European influences. Wissler took little cognizance of these
historical facts.

The American historical point of view had some inter-
esting internal contradictions. It was scientific in outlook,
but viewed central theories as suspect and tended to reject

even the search for laws and regularities, as well as to deny those theories developed by the evolutionists. Its theoretical predilections were for historical explanations, for demonstrating the current behavior of a people as the product of continuing tradition and outside influences, yet its scholars often did not examine the historical records which were available to them. It sought, rather, to infer history from ethnological evidence. It was empirical in approach, but this meant "letting the facts speak for themselves" rather than endeavoring to set up rigorous tests by which to validate their position. To all these statements, exceptional cases could be found, yet the above generalizations hold for most of American anthropological scholarship through the first thirty years of the century.

Nevertheless, the anthropologists engaged in these historical analyses demonstrated clearly that there were both minor and massive errors in evolutionary formulations. They demonstrated, for instance, that the presumed intermediary of a bronze age between a stone and an iron age was not found in Africa. They showed that the Hawaiian society (presumed to have maintained atavistic remnants of a primordial system of marriage) was in fact far advanced in matters of horticulture and political organization.

The empirical bias and the historical interest had one further positive advantage. It required detailed data from all known peoples; therefore the students in America spent a great deal of time in the field and while with their tribes, recorded all aspects of culture that came under their view and of which they could think to ask questions. The older school of anthropological theorists rarely went among tribes to study the cultures firsthand, and rarely were themselves active archeologists. The empirical orientation of American anthropology—perhaps furthered by the do-it-yourself attitude in American culture—placed first-rank scholars among the living primitives and resulted in massive vol-

umes of detailed cultural material, often suffused with far
greater insight and understanding than one would assume
from reading the theoretical presentations of the very same
scholars.

Other historical schools developed, using different methods and different systems of explanation and infused with
different ideas. Some of these may be viewed as merely
foolish, such as the theories of G. Eliot Smith and W. J.
Perry that all cultures were fundamentally the variant
decadent products of the influence of Egypt upon aboriginal savages. Others deserve more honor, such as the
Kulturkreislehre, which had a wide following in Europe,
though its importance is waning. This school sought generalized human history not as an evolutionary sequence but
rather as a historical development of a series of separate
culture entities, or circles, each of which developed in one
place and spread over a portion of the earth, maintaining
a measure of unity and continuity. This school, presumably
out of deep religious conviction, is largely anti-evolution-
istic and remains basically concerned with the philosophical
implications of the original condition of man. The late
Father Wilhelm Schmidt, for instance, was concerned with
aboriginal ideas concerning a belief in a High God, probably under the assumption that the universality of faith
offers a measure of scientific validation of monotheistic
theology.

These distinctions in historical systems may be laid aside.
The fundamental point is that there is a historical explanation of man's differences: a theory that the behavior of a
given people at a given time is the momentary end product
of a chain of events dating back in time, molded only inci-
dentally by environmental considerations. Neither their
divergent methodologies nor their different interpretations
of historic sequence are of concern here. It is, however,

important to recognize that history is fundamentally different from evolution as a system of explanation, though each of them is concerned with temporal sequence. We shall return to this shortly.

THE SOCIOLOGICAL ORIENTATION

What we are here calling the sociological point of view has only indirectly to do with the discipline of sociology. Rather, it is a view of human behavior that derives the nature of custom and action from the requirements of social life rather than from history, evolution, or psychology. In its purest form, it avoids the concept of culture entirely and sees the institutions of social action and the patterns of behavior as functioning to preserve the integrity of the body politic. Most sociological orientations have been labeled *functionalist,* in view of their concern with the workings of society and the functions performed by the institutional elements.

The line of descent of the sociological school derives ultimately from Auguste Comte, the French philosopher of the first half of the nineteenth century, via Emile Durkheim and the French sociological school that developed just prior to World War I. The French group was so heavily reduced by the losses of that war that it did not remain a major intellectual force. But its central conceptualizations were taken over by A. R. Radcliffe-Brown in England and have become the most important intellectual orientation of anthropology in that country since the early thirties. The point of view was a rejection of the atomistic character of postwar anthropology, which was tending to lose sight of individual cultures and human behavior in its search for the history of cultural elements. (This has never

been true, of course, of the field worker who is reporting
on an individual tribe; it applies only to theoretical writings and efforts at broad "explanations.")

The functionalist position sees the society as an operating mechanism or organism, and indeed permits analogy
between society and organic life. It takes as primary the
postulate that institutions function to unite individuals
into a more or less stable social structure, providing stable
interrelations among its constituent members and an adaptation to the environment such as will make possible an
ordered social life continuing through time. The second
postulate is that societies, as natural systems, are subject
to scientific laws; that is, that regularities may be established in the functioning of institutions so that one may
say: if A, then B. The effort on this score has produced
little result to date.

A major contribution to anthropology provided by the
sociological approach in England has been the development of detailed and elaborate monographs on particular
peoples, for the requirement in analysis is a thorough
knowledge of the specific people involved. In particular,
the sociological orientation has forced recognition of an
important aspect of human behavior. The earlier anthropologists started with the concept of custom, and viewed
culture as the sum of the traditions and customs of a
people. Unfortunately, however, people do not always follow their customs—as Kinsey's reports show so clearly for
America—and the distinction between actual behavior
and the body of customs is important to appreciate. The
social anthropologists are also concerned with customary
behavior (the norms of the social system), but they are far
more concerned with the interrelations of various aspects
of culture, the workings of the social mechanism. In this
analysis they have come to understand the relation between
actual behavior and the normative pattern and even to

appreciate what might be considered the norms of noncompliance. In this way, a better insight into the actual operation of primitive behavior in vivo has been obtained.

Furthermore, the approach has established the fact that social forms do serve general (and necessary) functions. Thus, to take an example early expressed by Radcliffe-Brown, the initiatory rites of the Andaman Islanders cannot be appreciated merely as a body of tradition handed down through time nor as the fortuitous borrowing from neighboring tribes, nor as the expression of a stage in the natural evolution of human religion. Rather, they are an institutional mechanism designed to communicate the social transition of youth to adulthood, to inculcate in the neophyte adults the primary values of their society and the exigencies of adult life, and to make public their new status. To take another example, clans are not merely an outgrowth of a family system in some early or intermediate stage in the evolution of human society nor are they the peculiar historic development of some region; rather, they are corporate entities functioning to preserve the integrity of a social group, to maintain the balance of power among sectors of the society, and to give legal and economic support to their component members. These institutions have a function; they contribute to the working of society.

Another major emphasis in the sociological approach to anthropological data has been supplied by Bronislaw Malinowski, of Polish birth, but long resident in England. This approach emphasized less the function than the integration of cultures. Malinowski probably knew the Trobriand Islanders, a Melanesian people, in greater detail than any major trained anthropologist has known the subjects of his investigations, and his writings have largely been based on this single society. His literary ability, his prolific writings, and his acquaintance with a broad range of theory enabled him to make a strong impact on anthropological thought. According to Malinowski, culture was the means of satisfying the basic life needs of human beings, and each culture was an integrated whole. Therefore, the provenience of an idea or custom was unimportant compared to the manner in which the culture transmuted it to its own requirements. Furthermore, the various aspects of culture were so intertwined that it was folly to treat each of them separately, as both evolutionists and historically oriented anthropologists tended to do. How could one understand religion without knowing social organization, economics without knowing the system of status?

The work of Ruth Benedict, whose *Patterns of Culture* undoubtedly is the most widely read anthropological work in America, may be included in this category—but with some difficulty. She shares with Radcliffe-Brown, and particularly with Malinowksi, an emphasis upon the integratedness of culture, i.e., the view of the whole society. But her treatment is more influenced by psychological modes of thought; the mechanistic orientation of Radcliffe-Brownian functionalism is alien to her viewpoint. She studies culture, not specific institutions. Perhaps it would be best to consider her as an entirely separate category.

Benedict was influenced by German philosophy and by her personal background as a poet; to her, the notion of unity was not sociological, it was spiritual. In her view, each culture has a pattern that can be characterized in terms of its dominant motif, and the pattern selects and molds the individual in terms of fitness for this dominant mode. In her efforts to characterize the essential spirit of cultures, Benedict carried the holistic point of view to its extreme; her position is less amenable to scientific ordering than to humanistic understanding; her personal insight gave her characterizations more validity than her methodology could demonstrate. In her analysis she uses words like *pattern* and *theme,* borrowed from aesthetics, rather than figures of speech taken from the sciences. Indeed, her treatment of culture makes the several institutions fit the patterned whole in a kind of Platonic aesthetic.

PSYCHOLOGICAL EXPLANATIONS

Anthropology and psychology have not generally been in close rapport. Early writers examined the psychology of primitive man, but they had little influence on the main current of anthropological thought. The only widely read general writer on primitive psychology is Lucien Lévy-Bruhl, a French scholar whose major works were done early in this century. His distinction between primitive prelogical mentality and the rational thought of civilized man is used more as a foil than as a model. Anthropology in England was early influenced by psychology, but the earlier psychological orientation has contributed little to the mainstream of anthropological thought.

The anthropologists' lack of interest in psychological theory may be laid to their lack of interest in the individual. Despite broader claims, anthropology has been overwhelmingly concerned with group activity and customary behavior. Theoretical orientations which endeavor to examine the evolution of society or the history of culture elements or the interrelationship between social institutions do not concern themselves much with the individual as such, and even less with his inner dynamics. When Paul Radin published *Crashing Thunder* (1926), the autobiography of a Winnebago Indian, this was an innovation; yet the work was largely hailed as giving a better insight into culture rather than as a contribution to psychology.

To be sure, anthropology requires some psychological

theory. For the most part, anthropologists have been willing to let matters rest with accepting a few broad assumptions about human psychology (more often implicit than explicit): that mankind everywhere is fundamentally the same; that physiological differences are not responsible for the manifest differences in human behavior in various cultures; that it is useless to speak of "human nature," since everywhere man's physiological characteristics are submerged in his culture; that the individual could be explained by his cultural environment, and not the other way about.

Between the two World Wars a new rapprochement developed between the fields, largely in relation to psychoanalytic theory. Freud himself turned to anthropology in an effort to account for the Oedipus complex, which he laid to a primordial act in which the jealous sons killed the father for the love of their mother—a kind of myth of aboriginal sin. Though anthropology was not drawn to this type of explanation, there did rapidly emerge an interest in the cultural aspect of psychodynamics. This interest was early developed in the writings of Edward Sapir and in the field work of Margaret Mead. Interest in psychology has grown in the past quarter century.

The central problem is this: since the infant at birth is culturally interchangeable, what happens to him in the process of growing up that makes him fit the demands of his own culture and reject those of any other? Margaret Mead particularly focused on this problem, showing how the growing-up process set the pattern for the character of adolescent problems, and in her New Guinea research showing that the fundamental personality traits which we define as masculine and feminine are not inherent but are a matter of cultural training. All anthropologists, of course, recognize that individuals at birth are culturally interchangeable, that culture is transmitted postnatally, though they might not agree with Mead that certain behavioral aspects are cultural rather than natural.

Anthropologists with psychological orientation focused their attention upon the child-rearing process and tried to see the conscious and unconscious training as the force which created the existing culture. Taking their dictum from Freudian psychology, that the first five years of life lay down the basic patterns of individual behavior, they examined the earliest experiences: the birth ritual itself, toilet training and sphincter control, feeding, handling, reward and punishment, and the establishment of patterned relations between the individual and his immediate social environment. If there is a rigid program of toilet training in the early months of life, then the people will be restrictive, parsimonious, and strait-laced, and the institutions of their society will reflect these personality attributes. But if children are raised in a congenial and warm atmosphere, are given personal attention and body contact with parents and others, then the general interpersonal relationships between individuals in that society will be warm; there will be a free expression of love and affection among its members. It was in this theoretical context that research was initiated. The major pioneer effort emerged from collaboration between an anthropologist, Ralph Linton, and a psychoanalyst, Abram Kardiner. After examination of a series of cultures they formulated the concept of the basic personality, which was seen, by Kardiner at least, as continuing unmodified through great stretches of time: in Western civilization from the beginning of Judeo-Christian history.

One result of this orientation has been to investigate depth psychology in other cultures, using such projective techniques as the Rorschach ink-blot cards and the Thematic Apperception Test, which are designed to reveal the hidden springs of human motivation—in Freudian terms, the unconscious. That response patterns differ is clear, and on theoretical grounds it seems likely that the content of the unconscious and the organization of personalities would differ among cultures. But massive problems stand in the way of this kind of research. The unconscious patterns which may differentiate peoples are overlaid with manifest cultural attributes and can be uncovered only through the use of language, itself an element of culture.

Whatever one's psychological predilection, whether it be orthodox Freudian psychoanalytic theory or Hullian conditioning, it is possible to accept the basic notion that practices of rearing children are strong determinants of the future behavior of the adult population. And it does not require much stretch of the imagination to see many aspects of a culture as fitting the needs of those common behavioral traits that have resulted from these uniformities in child training. A society that expects its adults to behave with elaborate and careful self-control will very likely place strict controls on its young, perhaps to protect the adults against flagrant breaches of conduct by the children which may involve the adults, perhaps out of the feeling that all persons should behave like adults as soon as they can, or perhaps to train them early for the culturally established expectation of adult life.

When, however, an attempt is made to give this approach greater specificity, to get down to particular institutions involving specific elements in infant care, then trouble arises. To continue with our example of the relation between self-control and child training we must go into more detail. One culture in which there is a strong emphasis upon self-control is that shared by the Hupa and Yurok Indians of northwestern California. According to psychoanalytic theory, the character traits of these people, which is miserly, suspicious, and much concerned with amassing wealth, should be associated with severe toilet-training practices. Eric Ericson, the Freudian scholar who studied the Yurok, said of them that "no student of psychoanalytic literature could avoid the impression that many of the Yurok 'traits' correspond to the 'anal character' as described by Freud and Abraham." Yet there is no evidence that toilet-training practices are severe; none which would make for a fixation on "the anal phase." There is, however, stern control of children by their parents, particularly with respect to eating.

Even if psychological theory dealing with the growth of the individual into his culture is fully accepted, it cannot explain the central problem of anthropology: the reasons for cultural variation. For the child-rearing practices themselves are part of the cultural picture, and the theory cannot demonstrate the forces that make for this variation. It cannot show why a particular pattern of child rearing has developed to create a personality matrix which will call forth certain institutions, except in terms of those institutions themselves; nor can it explain the institutions except in terms of the child-rearing practices that it asserts to be a response to them. This circular reasoning has been both the major fault and, paradoxically, one of the most important contributions of the psychological approach.

The reason for this is that the approach has reintroduced a concern with behavior itself. The quest for culture traits, social laws, and evolutionary formulas pays so much attention to the customary and the institutional that ongoing behavior often gets slight attention and the individual is lost sight of altogether. The discipline of anthropology had become guilty of treating the human being, to paraphrase Veblen's classic conception, as something that "oscillates like a homogeneous globule . . . under the influence of stimuli that shift him about . . . , but leave him intact." The question of whether culture resides in the individual or elsewhere is an old metaphysical debate which had best be laid aside. But the least that can be said is that culture does not exist without a personnel and that it manifests itself in the behavior of individuals. These individuals acquire (or progressively manifest) their culture as they grow from infancy into adulthood, and the dynamics of this growth process are inevitably a part of the total picture of human behavior. The ultimate understanding of social systems will require a recognition of the dynamic relationship between the ongoing institutions and the recruitment of infants into society.

ECLECTICISM

The foregoing endeavor to give the several basic orientations of anthropological thought in capsule form was made because it is necessary to appreciate the variety and character of the existing explanations for the divergent social systems. I am fully aware how inadequately the statements summarize even the major tenets of the several schools of thought. They completely ignore the overtones; they avoid the internal variations and the many subtle differences and involvements that have been a part of anthropological controversy over the past century. It is easy to show that any prolific scholar has taken contradictory stands, that there are areas of agreement between divergent viewpoints and strong differences within the separate schools. Yet scholarly behavior being what it is, the literature of anthropology is made up not only of assertions but of denials and rejections as well. The theorist is frequently unwilling merely to establish the validity of a position; he finds it necessary to refute the validity of others. The sociologically oriented tend to deny the historic explanations of social phenomena and to reject the psychological; and the same can be said of each for each.

To an outside observer coming fresh to the field of anthropology, it must be self-evident that none of these explanations are in and of themselves wrong and, furthermore, that they can all be right at the same time. Invoking the blind men and their elephant, we become impressed not with the inadequacies of the analogy each man invoked, but rather with the sentiment that each expressed at the other's erroneous judgment. For inadequacy is inherent in the understanding of such complex phenomena as human behavior; there is room for many kinds of right answers, each partial. In the case of the several anthropological schools of thought—leaving out those theorists who have spun tales of explanation little removed from the *Just So Stories*—there is insight and understanding in each, and none wholly negates the other.

This situation has not gone unnoticed. Recent theoretical work has tended to recognize the interrelated aspects of the variant points of view. Julian Steward, in his efforts at formulating developmental laws of growth, especially for more advanced cultures, and in his efforts to define the ecological factors in the development of institutions in the desert area of America, has explicitly recognized that the various schools of thought are not in conflict, but are seeking divergent but mutually compatible aims. The functional analysis of several systems and the fact of historical influences on culture do not militate against the existence of regularities in evolutionary development. Steward's efforts to demonstrate regularities in the development of early civilization in Middle America, Peru, and the Old World contribute both to functional and evolutionary theory. The work of George P. Murdock and the development of the Human Relations Area Files at Yale share this eclectic attitude. Following a tradition from Edward Tylor, Murdock tries to correlate relationships between various aspects of social organization and to examine the possibilities of evolutionary sequence on a thoroughly empirical basis, without denying the validity of history or avoiding the sociological factors. Quite recently the detailed statistical analysis of *Indian Tribes of North America* by Harold E. Driver and William C. Massey, furthered this multiple approach to anthropological problems. They show by the statistical method of factor analysis that both evolutional-sociological and diffusional elements are requisite to explain the distribution of cultural features throughout native North America.

To cite one further example, the work of Clyde Kluckhohn has never been limited to a single orientation. Years of close collaboration in the interdisciplinary department of Social Relations at Harvard—particularly his close collaboration with Henry A. Murray (psychology) and Talcott Parsons (sociology)—has enhanced his broad intellectual outlook, so that sociological and psychological orientations are displayed along with his recognition of cultural-historical forces.

It is our purpose here to show that these separate orientations to human behavior are not in mutual conflict; that each has its proper sphere in the understanding of the human scene. Later, it will be pointed out that not only is each separately valid, but that true understanding requires each; that a proper sociological explanation requires psychological assumptions, and so on, each to each. But for the present, let us examine a single institution in terms of the several major orientations we have outlined: The modern system of state universities.

State-supported institutions of higher learning, as we will see in due course, are a major element in modern life; in focusing upon them we do not select an item of modern culture that is either insignificant or transitory. On the other hand, a quite specific example is an advantage—to speak of broader, and older, institutions such as the family or the church would take us too far afield.

The state university is not an old institution, but its roots are deep in history. Deriving from the intellectual tradition in America and the strong sentiment favoring freedom of opportunity, it nevertheless traces back in form and function to the older pattern of the privately endowed and religiously supported institutions. These in turn are patterned after the great institutions of England, France, and Germany, and ultimately go back to the scholastic orders and the monasteries of medieval Europe. Many traits of the academic tradition—the "sheepskin," the cap and gown, the "public" examination for higher degrees, the insistence on learning a foreign language; many of the very terms used, such as *schools* and *colleges, diplomas* and *degrees;* many of the special ceremonies observed, such as the baccalaureate address or the senate meeting, have a hoary antiquity. Truly the state universities are a product of a unique historical development. Yet they are not simply a product of history.

For the state universities comprise a social institution meeting social ends. Modern America, perhaps more than any other country, is a nation of technicians, each controlling a special area of knowledge and each, through the marketing of such knowledge, gaining his personal livelihood. Not only must there be recruitment and training of this professional personnel; there must also be, in a society that values the opportunity for personal advancement, the means by which any person with adequate native ability and initiative can acquire the training for such professional service. The training must be made broadly available; it must be relatively inexpensive. The free state university meets a need by providing this avenue of personal advancement in an environment dominated by technical proficiency. It serves other and lesser ends as well, offering opportunities for a semiprotected adult life for persons in postadolescence, an environment in which young men and women may find relatively congenial mates out of a heterogenous population, and the like. But these things need not detain us. The state university can be seen simply as a response to a manifest need of our modern social system functionally related to the economy, the family, and other institutions. But again, not so simply!

As every incoming freshman must repeatedly hear, the institution is not its buildings, its library, and its laboratories; it is the men and women, the administrators, the faculty, yes, even the students, that make it what it is. In less sonorous phrases, it is a social environment in the life cycle of the individual, responsive to those internalized demands that have been transmitted to youth in our culture. It is an environment for individuals imbued with a motivation to succeed, and it has elaborate sets of markers to show the progress of the individual through its hierarchy of years, similar to the growth charts on a doctor's wall and the blueprint for child development set forth by Dr. Arnold Gesell. Further, in a society in which comparative standards of excellence start with early child training, it offers a refined grading of achievement, recorded at least twice each year, and summarized and calculated to the second decimal point to give a precise evaluation of personal worth. Such a system of grading does not appear in the elite schools of Europe; it is a response to the freely mobile and highly competitive spirit of American culture. The state institutions of higher learning are a response to the personality needs of American youth. Surely such an institution could appear only in a culture where from infancy children hear themselves compared to others with

respect to precocity and strength, in a culture lacking in
formalized authority but requiring that the individual
seek the cultural goals out of an inner drive that derives
from his strong urge for advancement, rather than because
others force him to.

Yet the universities are a development that is part of the
evolution of society to its present superindustrial stage.
All societies provide training for their young. In a simple
technology this training can be provided within the family;
with somewhat more advanced technologies, some formalized system of apprenticeship may be necessary. Most
societies sufficiently large and complex to be formed into
political states have developed industrial arts that require
institutions of learning. But the institutions of higher
learning in pre-industrial states served to provide for the
transmission of cultural values and the indoctrination of
the young among the elite rather than to provide cadres of
technically trained personnel. With the emergence of modern industrial society, the body of highly skilled knowledge necessary to maintain the plant in production and
to create further technical proficiency requires a constant
large-scale program of recruitment and training of personnel and the progressive development of new technologies. We can see systems similar to our own emerging
elsewhere. As a matter of fact, a certain alarm has spread
in America over the rapidity with which the U.S.S.R.
has developed a comparable massive training program.
New countries, such as Indonesia, are trying to model their
higher learning after our own, and old countries, such as
England, are revamping their education to give it a broader
base in the population than was provided by traditional
colleges, remnants of that earlier stage of civilization. The
institution of state universities as a means for the mass
training of a technologically competent body of func-

tionaries can be seen as the simple end product of an
evolutionary process that started when the first father
showed his son how to haft a spear.

Obviously, this institution, and every other in any society,
can be seen in terms of any and all these explanatory
systems, for each is always in operation. The predilection
toward one or another will depend upon the particular
aspect of the human scene that the scholar chooses to
elucidate, upon whatever is congenial to his intellectual
predispositions. Those who are most interested in the
details of form will undoubtedly seek historical explanations; those interested in function, the sociological; those
interested in meaning, the psychological. Yet each aspect
is equally necessary for understanding the total phenomenon.

But the point should be carried further. It is not only
that each orientation should be tolerant of the other, that
those who seek psychological explanation should give the
sociologists their due. It is, rather, that each kind of explanation *requires* the others; that, say, in order to understand a phenomenon sociologically requires a proper psychological orientation, and so on.

All these systems of explanation must necessarily be
brought to bear if we are adequately to comprehend man's
social behavior. In this book we shall recognize the validity
of each mode of explanation, but the major emphasis will
be upon the sociological and evolutionary contributions
to the understanding of man's way.

III

The Social Imperatives

GENERAL CHARACTER OF SOCIAL ORGANIZATION

IF A SOCIETY is to persist, it must have certain characteristics. These we shall call the *social imperatives*. The purpose of this chapter is to explore the nature of these imperatives.

The specific fulfillment of these imperative social demands varies from one culture to another. This variation is not haphazard, but rather is influenced by the underlying mode of economic production which places specific limits and conditions on the fulfillment of the social imperatives. The theoretical basis for this second postulate is the subject of the next chapter.

To appreciate the operation of the social imperatives, we must first examine a series of central and interrelated theoretical points:

1. Man is everywhere committed to social life, a fact which involves him in social interrelationships.

2. The commitment to social existence requires that orderly procedures be followed in these necessary interrelationships, an orderly procedure which we call the *social organization* of the community.

3. This orderly relationship must be clearly perceived by each member of the society.

4. The perception of this order is communicated to each individual as he grows into participation, normally in the process of growing up.

5. In this process of growing into the system, the individual translates his personal aims into socially acceptable modes of behavior, subordinating (under normal conditions) his personal ends to the requisites of the community, in so far as these are in conflict.

6. The individual accepts these social ends through the reward and punishment system, operating primarily on the individual's need for positive affect.

7. The social organization is therefore an on-going pattern of social interrelationships continuing through time, and may be thought of as a part of culture: as part of the shared experience of a population, learned and transmitted (with modification) through the generations.

8. This culturally derived social organization is not a freely developing product of historical change, but is subject to the limitations imposed upon it by the fact that it is an instrumentality for maintaining order.

9. The social organization must therefore be geared to self-maintenance of the community rather than to the satisfaction of the individual, though minimal needs of the individual must be met in order for that perpetuation to be accomplished.

10. The rule of perpetuation is self-policing, in that failure will lead either to the demise of the society or to the alteration of the social organization.

11. The necessary features of the social organization are what we call the *social imperatives*.

Having thus briefly stated the thesis, let us examine its major points in some detail before proceeding to the social imperatives themselves.

The first point in the syllogism has been expounded at some length in an earlier chapter: man's commitment to social life is implicit in the nature of man, existing outside cultural forces as such. The commitment is not biological in the simple sense of that term but in the sense that it is somehow an inevitable consequence of man's biological nature.

But if man is committed to living among his fellows, then there must be standard ways of behaving with respect to these others, some mode by which cooperative effort can be achieved, some means of resolving conflicts that arise, some anticipation of the behavior of others. This apparently is true of animal aggregates, such as herds and flocks and packs and troops of apes, though here without the involved symbol system and communication devices that are made possible by speech.

Each person must have some awareness of this social system, but not necessarily an understanding of its whole. More particularly, he must be aware of that part which impinges upon him, so that he can anticipate the actions of others and their expectations of him. That is to say, the grocer needs to understand his relation to the customer and the salesman, to the banker and the boxboy. He does not have to understand the operations of the market or the geopolitical considerations of national policy makers in order to make change or vend bananas. Each person gets his immediate awareness from the indoctrination he receives through the process of living in the social system, at first through parental socializing agents, but continuously in the normal intercourse of life. These basic premises are set for him early, in terms of patterned expectations; and it is in terms of these basic premises and their constant reinterpretation that he normally operates. Therefore, by the time he can act independently, he is not merely committed to social existence but to a particular pattern of social behavior, to particular expectations of the behavior of other persons and to their expectations of him. Thus he is living in a social organization that is a cultural heritage.

Each person must adjust to the society in which he is to live. His commitment to it demands something of him; he cannot freely operate in terms of personal whim and self-satisfaction. This is no stand against the Great Man Theory of history, which deserves some modified support—for cultures do change, and the actions of men, wittingly or unwittingly, are responsible for such change. It is rather the recognition that most of the people all the time and all the people most of the time conform to expectations set by the patterned life around them. Social life may be seen as a bargain in which the individual subordinates himself to customary demands and receives in turn a social environment in which to operate; whether or not it is a good bargain, it is written into the commitment to social existence.

Although social organization is a cultural heritage, it is not the end product of whimsical forces, taking any direction that the turn of fortune provides. It is subject rather to the dictates of survival. These dictates include the need to nurture its personnel, at least sufficiently to enable its continued procreation, to order its internal relations so that there may be sufficient amity to allow for the orderly satisfaction of man's inevitable wants, and to protect itself from the vicissitudes of an external environment made up not only of resources and predators, but of other social orders that stand as a potential threat to its continuance. It is this circumstance that makes the term *imperative* appropriate in speaking of the universal aspects of social organization, and by which the word *must* is justified. This must is not a moral must, carrying with it some notion of an eternal verity; nor is it an inevitable must, unconditionally guaranteed. It is rather Hobson's must, the choice (figuratively speaking) between fulfillment or demise; the must of *sine qua non,* for without these features the society does not continue. We shall return to this in the next chapter, for it is also a matter crucial to the understanding of evolutionary development.

How quickly such forces operate is not a matter that can yet be established. To argue by analogy, we know that man must eat to live, but we know that he does not eat at every moment; we know that he can survive for extended periods of time without food, depending upon other aspects of his condition and the nature of his environment. If physiological rigors can be flouted, it stands to reason that social demands, too, can temporarily be held in abeyance. Here we therefore need to use those phrases familiar in economics: *in the long run* and *by and large.* Such limitation does not vitiate our premise; it gives recognition only to the fact that other forces are also at work and may obscure the issue. The must in our premise means that, in time, a social system failing to meet the requisite elements will undergo such alteration that it will meet them, its personnel will be reorganized into new social systems, or the population will be submerged or wiped out by some other system—the length of time required depending upon the seriousness of the lack, the substitutive forces brought to play, and the external factors that are a threat or a support to the system.

With these considerations in mind, we can now turn to the social imperatives. The universal and imperative components for all social systems, however primitive or civilized they may be, are: groups, values, status, role, authority, and ideology. By *groups* we mean the formation of social entities within which there is a sense of commonality among members, a felt distinction between members and outsiders, and an internal structure. By *values* is meant those recognized qualities that persons in the society should possess and the symbolic representations by which these desirable qualities are given overt expression. The term *status* denotes the position of persons (and of groups) within the total configuration of the society, the standing of persons relative to other persons. *Role* combines the attitude, behavior, and sentiments that are appropriate to particular statuses and are expected of those persons who hold them. *Authority* is the recognized relationship involving the legitimate power of decision making over certain areas of the conduct and activities of other members of the society. *Ideology* is the system of beliefs that offers an understanding of the established social order: the intellectual and spiritual rationale for the social *status quo*.

Needless to say, these several components are closely interrelated in their operation in any social system, and it would be legitimate to view each as a facet of the generalized concept: social organization. Let us examine the manifestations of each.

GROUPS

The universal existence of groups is perhaps the most evident of all the components of a social system. It is necessary, however, to appreciate the meaning of groups in the conduct of human affairs and to examine their nature and variety.

All human beings normally enter their first group—the family—at the moment of birth, and in the course of a lifetime become part of many such social entities. Their size may vary from the dual relationship of a childless family to a loose and massive social system such as a modern political party. It is proper to consider society as a whole to be a group—the largest group containing within it all the other groups.

What does "groupness" consist in? First, members of a group sense their unity and commonality. There is a felt distinction between the personnel of the group and the outsider, a kind of psychological membrane which marks those within from those outside. This barrier may be virtually impenetrable, as the castes of India or the clans of many primitive tribes. It may be relatively open, as the membership of the American Anthropological Association, which requires no more than the payment of a small fee and the expression of interest.

Second, each group must have a focus of interest. This may be no more than the collection of strange customs of exotic peoples, but it could be as important as the maintenance of power and authority over a large territory. With such common interest come certain common activities, which again may be far-reaching or slight, depending upon the circumstances. People do not form a group merely by being together but rather by sharing interests and engaging in activity to further the interests of the group. Indeed, in our modern system of communication often the members of a group are not physically together and, in fact, the same can be said of primitive clans, as we shall see.

Finally, groups are organized. There is an internal structure, a distinction of statuses and roles, lines of communication, and foci of authority. This is obviously true of the larger groups in modern American society, but it is equally true of the simple and informal groups that we call cliques. William F. Whyte clearly demonstrated the existence of a firm structure in the apparently transitory gangs of Boston slum youths; and in his novel, *The Ox-Bow Incident,* Walter Van Tilburg Clark took pains to show that the mob that did the lynching was closely organized, with a leader and a couple of lieutenants organizing even so short-lived a group.

When we examine groups from a variety of social systems, we can recognize three separate, general bases for group formation. The first form is the *familistic,* where the central unity and the basis of membership depends upon ties of kinship. Which ties are considered important, how large such groups become, and what their functions are differ from one society to another, but all social systems have familistic groups. The second general type is *spatial.* Spatial groups are based upon persons having a common dwelling place or area. Our towns, counties, states, and nations may be viewed as territorial groups, and our membership rests fundamentally on residence, though other criteria may be brought into consideration. Third, groups may be formed merely on the basis of some special interest or activity irrespective of space or kinship. A group unified for purposes of some common recreation, such as a society for ham radio operators; a group brought together for some kind of economic activity, such as a union; or a group brought together for certain kinds of prestigeful activities, such as the secret societies found in Melanesia and on the American plains or in a modern college, are all examples of this last type. Most, but not all, societies have such social units. In some primitive societies, it is possible to get the world's work done in the context of familistic and spatial grouping.

One important attribute of groups is the manner in which membership is attained. Sociologists usually make distinctions between those groups in which membership is foreordained by some circumstance beyond the control of the person himself, and those in which the individual can freely choose to select or reject affiliation. The former have sometimes been called groups of common origin and the

latter, groups of common interest; but the terminology
is unfortunate because all groups have a common interest.
We shall distinguish them as *ascribed groups* and *volitional
groups*. Since no one has the power to choose his parents,
the family into which he is born is always an ascribed
group. In the modern world, nationality is usually ascribed;
in American society, the social involvements of racial affiliation are ascribed. Some primitive societies have volitional
groups, but some appear not to have. The evolution of
society from the simple to the complex appears to bring
with it a shift in emphasis from ascribed to volitional
groups.

The choice of membership in a volitional group is not
entirely free. An individual may be rejected from membership or there may be very strong pressures on him to join.
The former is readily illustrated by exclusive clubs, the
latter by such occupational association as the American
Medical Association, for its influence on medical services
and facilities makes it almost mandatory for a doctor to
maintain his membership if he wishes to practice.

This matter of volition has some important implications
for the character of the group. Where a group is foreordained—and there are societies in which a person is a
group member from before his birth until the last memory
of him disappears—it can maintain an assumption of unity
that is not available to a group whose members are free
to move in and out. It is not that the unity is greater
but that the individual members are more completely
caught in group demands, which are inescapable and therefore potentially more autocratic.

Groups perform functions in society, and each group
normally has a manifest function. The manifest function
of the family is procreation and the maintenance of the
physical and economic satisfactions of its component members; the function of a union is the protection and further-

ance of mutual interest; a social club functions to provide recreation for its members. It is within the context of group life that the world's work is done. But the group also frequently performs one or more of a second set of functions, latent functions, which relate to the needs of its individual members.

One of these is that the group functions as a body through which the cultural attitudes or special social demands and expectations are communicated to the individual. The child acquires his culture first through his family; the scholar acquires a knowledge of professional ethics, special terminology, and the construct of ideas, through the organization of academicians with which he associates. The fraternity brother learns the secret signs and symbols, and the express values of his group. A second function is that the group gives the individual strength; it supports him in his behavior and assures him of the propriety of his actions and attitudes. This can be particularly seen with such deviant groups as nudists, who as individuals would be acting immorally as well as illegally, but who as members of the group are engaged in activities which are both morally sanctioned and legally admissible. Indeed, some state laws have distinguished the psychopath from the religious cult leader arbitrarily by the size of the group of followers he can claim! Finally, the group provides a social matrix in which the individual satisfies his need for positive affect. It is within the matrix of smaller social entities that people get personal responses of affection, prestige, and status; it is within the context of the group that they satisfy these needs.

Other animals live in social aggregates but it is doubtful if any other animal has something that can be called "social groups" except the total herd or flock, and even these probably may not have the psychological characteristics that are part of the human group. Separation of this kind is found among the social insects, but the basis of distinction is so thoroughly biological that it is quite improper to make analogies with mammalian social systems.

Human societies are everywhere made up of numerous groups and it is important to give some consideration to the relationships that may exist between the different groupings in a social system. Groups may be distinguished as between those which are *mutually exclusive* and those which are *overlapping*. In the former case, membership in one group precludes membership in another, as for example the castes of India. Where clan systems prevail, if a person belongs to one clan, he usually cannot be a member of another. Many societies are made up of a mosaic of separate but comparable groups. These groups may be coequal with one another in power or prestige, or they may be hierarchical. Clans are generally coequal, castes hierarchical.

By overlapping groups we mean groups in which the membership of one includes or may include members from another. These in turn can be divided into two kinds. If all members of one group are included within the broader group, this relationship is referred to as *inclusive*. Thus, for instance all the persons in any one state are also members of the United States. In primitive societies there frequently exist lineages, the members of which are also members of a larger and more inclusive clan made up of several lineages, and these in turn may be included in a yet larger group. The other kind of overlapping is called *noninclusive*. Under these conditions, membership in one neither establishes nor precludes membership in another, so that normally there are persons in one group who do and others who do not have membership in a second. Our system of clubs and associations is generally of this kind.

Membership in a group involves a measure of commitment, and group loyalties tend to organize sentiment in the society. In many social systems, as in clan-organized societies, the loyalty to special groups overrides the loyalty to the society, and the social system may even rest upon a balance of power between mutually exclusive coequal groups standing in opposition to one another. Where mutually exclusive groups are ordered hierarchically, prestige is a matter of group affiliation, and power usually goes with prestige. Where overlapping groups are inclusive, the sentiments of the larger are not generally in conflict with the smaller units but broadly subsume the more specific and more intimate ties. But where overlapping groups are noninclusive, where some members of one group belong to another and other members of the first do not, then group loyalties may truly come into conflict. Thus in modern society, where ties to neighborhood, church, occupation group, and fraternity are each individually contracted, the sentiments invoked by each may differ, and the group loyalties may draw the individuals apart rather than serve to reinforce one another and strengthen the sense of commitment.

VALUES

Every society provides a blueprint for propriety. The nature of that propriety, the sharpness of delineation, and the supports which give it strength vary from one society to another; but within each social system there are certain overriding unities with respect to the idea of what makes a good man, a true man, a respectable man.

The Greeks had a word for it. *Areté* was a term used in ancient Greece to refer to the proper qualities of a man of virtue. Greek culture had an extremely clear and explicit aristocratic tradition. All cultures have their own form of areté, even when they do not have a word for it.

Go to any tribe, however undeveloped, and you will be provided with ideas about the qualities that are expected of leaders, the features that make a man a good man or a bad man, a respectable or a disreputable one.

Values, then, may be defined primarily as those individual personal qualities which are considered to be desirable by people in a given culture. Industriousness and thrift are such values in our own society, though very nearly the opposite was valued in the antebellum South. Bravery, strength, perseverance, self-denial, artistic talent, self-control, aggressiveness, and a host of other traits, singly or in combination, can be regarded in a culture as desirable qualities. But values are more than vague, abstract attributes; they are also the patterns of behavior which are the manifestations of these values. Regular compliance with the obligations of one's job and a favorable bank balance are values in our society. Bravery in battle, equanimity in the face of physical threats, forgoing satisfactions for the sake of others, composing a sonnet, and so on, may all be considered aspects of value systems. Furthermore, the concept of values includes also the public and external expression of these attributes. Expenditures in the form of housing, clothes, and cars are public expression of the favorable bank balance that derives from industry and thrift and this, too, is a part of our value system. In every culture there are material things, titles, required expressions of deference, and the like, which are public and concrete manifestations of value attributes.

One may question a concept that covers so wide a range of phenomena, but it is justifiable. For people regularly read from one to another; that is, the cultures themselves make this confusion. We may consider the manifestations of the public expressions of values as mere symbols rather than the real values; and philosophically this is the case. But man takes his symbols seriously and, in fact, frequently treats the symbols as the primary reality, for reasons that have already been indicated. This point will recur shortly.

In any society, the values are set down by tradition, and values are naturally conservative. Values are culturally established; that is, they are a part of tradition and are inculcated in the process of growing up. The deeper seated and presumably more basic values are acquired without awareness and are held without self-consciousness. They may be different for men and women, and there may be differing values for different classes or categories within the social system, but certain values are generally held by all members, though they may not be attainable by all.

The character of the value system will generally reflect certain basic needs of the social system in the context of its environment and technology. Thus, for instance, bravery and fortitude on the plains of North America were meaningful in the context of the highly fluid military situation that developed after the acquisition of the horse by the Plains Indians. A kind of stoic religious virtue and a strong emphasis on community solidarity upheld the Pueblo Indians of the Southwest in an extremely harsh environmental context where a high degree of solidarity was required to stave off the combined forces of drought and aggressive military neighbors. The essential value of self-determination that charactizes the modern American culture is related to the continuing expansion of our economy, first across the physical frontier and now across the technological frontiers that have made physical and social mobility a desirable quality and, for many, a necessity.

Such clear integration with manifest aspects of the economy is not always found; since values are conservative, they can become out of joint with the times. But by and large, the virtues which a society recognizes are related to the circumstances in which it operates.

The existence of values is a social imperative; the form they take is functionally related to other aspects of the social situation, handed down, with modification, through time. But these values are sought for and possessed by individuals. From the standpoint of the individual, he has or does not have those values which his society cherishes. This Plains Indian is less brave than that one; this Northwest Coast Indian has the greater capacity to give; this American is the better salesman. From the individual standpoint, values are therefore seen to be differentiating. They mark one man off from another within an established cultural context. The important thing is to realize that each culture has a set, or sets, of values, but that each individual (for one reason or another) possesses these qualities in greater or lesser degree.

The values by which people live are symbolized: there are techniques by which an individual's virtue is publicized to the community as a whole. Usually, if not in every case, certain specific things or acts are seen as desiderata and indicate the holding or achievement of virtue. As already noted, in our society such symbolization is represented by money and, by extension, the things which money can buy that make one's circumstances different or "better." Whatever creature comforts are satisfied by the possession of the gadgets of modern life, these gadgets are, nevertheless and always, a symbolic representation of achievement in a society where self-responsibility dominates the value patterns. It is very much the same among the Plains Indians where stealing horses, striking but not killing an enemy (*counting coup,* in anthropological terminology), and other military honors were symbolic representations of masculine achievement, demonstrating the virtues which dominated these militaristic social systems. In the southwestern part of North America, with its heavy emphasis upon religious virtue, leadership in and knowledge of religious activities represent the attainment of Hopi or Zuni areté.

We noted earlier man's peculiar capacity to symbolize, and repeat that this quality seems to be a very part of human nature. One of the insistent features of man's symbolization is that symbol and reality become so intertwined and unified in the thought of the people that they are not easily separated: one cannot readily determine what is symbol and what reality. Ask a Plains Indian what makes a good man, and he may tell you bravery; he may tell you "counting coup." We have treated values as the desirable qualities in human character as defined by the culture, but these inevitably are vaguely expressed qualities: abstract, intellectual, and rather remote from the activities of daily life. The symbolic elements are titles, memberships, rituals of deference, forms of dress and adornment, possessions: the concrete attributes which have more dramatic effect upon the personnel of the culture.

From the social standpoint, values give unity to the culture and to the society. They form a rallying point around which action takes place. From the standpoint of the individual, the symbols act as motivating forces that tend to channelize individual behavior. It is just as easy to tell a youngster that he should be diligent because that is the proper character of a man (in our culture) as it is to say that he should work diligently in order to have the things that he wants. But clearly the latter is the more effective means of communication; the symbol is a more forceful goad to action and acquiescence than is the invisible reality for which it stands.

Values may be achieved or ascribed. It is a tenet of the American middle-class culture that the values may be acquired by any individual and that any individual can make of himself whatever he wishes. This is one of the central qualities of our social mobility. In our system, the achievement of the cultural values by any individual is considered a matter of his own ability and energy. Some people in our society feel that equal ability is given to all and that success is merely a matter of application, while others think ability varies, but is established through hard work; but whichever emphasis is accepted, the individual is held responsible for achieving the values on his own. Ours is not the only culture which places this emphasis upon the individual's own responsibility; it seems to recur in all stages of social development, though it is perhaps more frequent in very primitive societies living closer to the exigencies of life than where highly organized social behavior acts as a buffer between man's abilities and his desires.

In many other societies, the person inherits the value symbols and by implication the virtue that goes with them. This is the rationale underlying any clearly demarcated class system, such as the estates in earlier European society, and more sharply the caste system of India. There are other foreordained values, too, to be found in the societies of the world: to be the first-born son of a first-born son, to be born with a caul, to be heir to a title. No society, to be sure, is ever so clearly given either to ascription of values as to make any change impossible or to the achievement of values as to allow absolutely unfettered changes through personal actions. America has its first families and native sons; and India is not entirely devoid of social mobility. But the dominant mode and the cultural assumptions vary greatly.

Values, it was noted, may be considered as naturally conservative. By "naturally" we have reference not to human nature but to social nature. That is, there are forces in the social system which tend to preserve the established value pattern, especially its symbolic aspects. Established values in any culture are held differentially by its members.

Those who hold values are given prestige in the community, for such is the nature of any value system. Persons of prestige tend to have power to influence the behavior of others, both directly by exerting pressure and by weighting the decisions for their community, and indirectly by serving as models for the remainder of the population, particularly the young. People with prestige will not normally do things that would undermine the system of values in which they are enjoying an advantage, but will consciously or unconsciously try to preserve both the underlying realities of human attributes and their symbolic representation. In short the values and the influences for their continuation form one eternal round. The inertia of a value is such that even new groups coming into power by revolution generally reassert the old symbols of value and arrogate them to themselves. Yet it is possible for values, as for any other part of a culture, to change. There is a tendency for them to change under the pressure of such forces as the development of new technologies, the acquisition of new territories, the appearance of new enemies. In other words, external circumstances alter the life conditions of the people and so may bring change in their values. Both the continuity and the forces for change deserve illustration.

The Belgian historian Henri Pirenne, in his analysis of medieval cities, shows that "those who were the beneficiaries of the established order were bent upon defending it not so much, perhaps, because it guaranteed their interest as because it seemed to them indispensable to the preservation of society." At the same time, the merchants who sought change were not overthrowing a system but demanding concessions to make their functions operative.

Among the Hupa Indians of northwestern California, European influence brought in agriculture. Several Hupa took to farming. Some of these were the sons of white men, illegitimate children, according to old Hupa ideas, and therefore tainted, according to native values, with a bar sinister which prevented their participation in ceremonial life. But as these farmers prospered, they purchased the religious paraphernalia which served as the major value symbols in old Hupa life, thereby not only attaining prestige in the old system of values, but also preserving the function of these ancient symbols. The force of old value attitudes may hamper culture change.

When the Blackfoot Indians were taught farming and given farm equipment by the Canadian government, the project was a dismal failure, for it required types of activity that ran contrary to Blackfoot values: sedentary life, a hard daily routine, emphasis on the separateness of the individual household, and husbanding of resources rather than a pattern of general sharing and generosity. When cattle were introduced, however, the Blackfoot elite took to the new symbol which so closely resembled the keeping of horses, which had been the former chief value symbol.

The industrial revolution had similar influences on European life. The new mode of production, made possible first through commerce with the outside world and later by the harnessing of power, offered a new source of the wealth and power which previously had rested chiefly on ownership of land and military leadership. As a result, a new class of elite emerged. But many of the old symbols are retained, and the peerage continues, empty of power and augmented regularly by the "elevation" of persons to titles actually several centuries out of tune with the times.

A most important aspect of the concept of values is closely related to our postulate of a need for positive affect. The individual comes into being devoid of value orientations but with a tendency to respond to the cues of his environment in ways that will best serve his basic needs. Among these needs is the desire for response from his fellow beings.

Gradually he internalizes the values through the cues given in response to his action. If the system of values is clear and coherent, then the forces bringing about the internalization of values are strong and he accepts both the cultural postulates for behavior and the desire for the symbols which are attainable. To be sure, he receives verbal instructions and hortatory declamations as well, but these are later and secondary bases for learning. The deeper lying attitudes are acquired with the same subtlety with which he acquires the nuances of the speech around him; that is, without awareness of the assumptions, without conscious model. There is another means by which these values are inculcated, or rather an extension of the above: in later life, as youth and adult, the rewards provided for the fulfillment of expectations must be in accord with the established pattern of values. Personal breakdown—and societal breakdown, especially where rapid social changes are taking place —often occurs where the expectations established in achieving affectional response as a child do not provide a basis for reward in later years. The psychological involvements in the communication of values represent a very important aspect of anthropological understanding, but it is peripheral to our present interests. What is important, however, is that values are acquired by the individual through responses he gets from his social environment in his efforts to seek positive affect. Values, it may be said, are the culturally channeled means of seeking positive affect.

There is an extension of this point. In any small social unit the individual is personally known; the qualities he possesses and the values he manifests are matters of general knowledge. As the group expands, the direct personal contact becomes attenuated, and response to the individual is increasingly in symbolic or secondary terms. This distinction can be seen in our own society by comparing the intimate group of family or clique as against larger social entities such as the community. For this reason secondary symbols are more important in large societies than in small primitive bands. And it is in this sense that the seeking after positive affect is diverted to the ends of achieving the symbols of prestige. This is true to the extent that the symbol may so completely replace the reality element that the individual often cuts himself off from the opportunity for direct personal responses. He is diverted, one might say, from direct access to human response by the cultural demands to behave in accordance with the symbol system. This is the case for some of the West African kings, who were literally prisoners of the tabus which surrounded them, unable to enjoy free human contacts. It has also been said to be the case of the successful modern organization man, in his empyrean heights, cut off from the give-and-take of the more normal human intercourse of his fellows. Although the individual always has personal contacts with family and neighbors, his behavior may cut off the very warm relations that we assume stand as basic human desires. But this should not surprise us, for all human needs are transmitted into cultural needs, and in the process the satisfaction of the need can itself be subverted.

STATUS AND ROLE

Interpersonal relationships are ordered, in that each person relates to each other in ways that are fairly standardized, depending upon their relative positions. This concept of position which we regularly employ in conversation about people in society has been formalized in sociological thought under the term *status*. Status, therefore, may be defined as the positions of a person vis-à-vis others. And a social system may be regarded as a set of standard positions that interrelate all members of the community.

Status has a specific as well as a generalized aspect. The specific element in status appears in direct face-to-face relationships, in the actual and direct contact between persons: the boss to the employee, the son to the father, the priest to the communicant. Generalized statuses refer to the broader concept of relations in the social system as a whole: employees, minors, priests. In every society these generalized positions have their direct implications for immediate social relationships; they also have their broader relevance in the general pattern of social action. Thus, for instance, the rights and obligations of minors in the United States are set forth in the law, while custom further dictates the specificities of such a relationship.

These rights and obligations, privileges and duties, that are the component parts of recognized statuses are the blueprints for behavior of persons holding them. They are spoken of as *roles,* a concept taken from the theater, where the role is an actor's particular behavior in a given context. The figure of speech is apt, for the role is not the action itself, but an indication of what the action should be. The actor must both learn and interpret his role; must behave within the limits set by it to the best of his ability. So, too, with social roles. That is to say, the father in our society is expected to advise, admonish, and (when necessary) chastise his son; he is expected to give him comfort and support, to provide for his needs, and to launch him toward a career. His advice may or may not be well phrased and well conceived; his punishments may be severe or harsh, timely or ill-timed; his support may be lavish or inadequate, depending upon his talents, wisdom, and economic circumstances. Only when the father manifestly oversteps the bounds of a proper interpretation of his role (brutality, failure to support) does society take formal cognizance of his behavior, though lesser transgressions of propriety (overindulgence, bad advice) may lead to criticism from family, friends, and neighbors. A particular role may be congenial to a person or it may not, and it is well known that people often have a status that they enjoy but dislike some of the aspects of the role they must play. A banker may very well enjoy the prestige that his status gives him but find it heartbreaking to deny a loan to a worthy but financially unsound enterprise; a professor may enjoy performing before his class but regard as onerous tasks the preparation of lectures or the need to fail students.

In every society there are statuses and roles, but the basis for status formulation varies from one culture to another and a similar status may have different roles. Thus in American society and in the Melanesian Trobriand society, the status of father is recognized. But the role component of a father's status is different: the Trobriand father does not chastise his son; he does not have the responsibility for the son's future success. He relates to the boy very much as the kindly uncle does in our society, lavishing affection and gifts on him but having no direct role in his rearing. At the same time, the boy's uncle—that is, the mother's brother, inasmuch as the Trobriand Islanders do not give the same status to the father's brother as they do the mother's—plays the role we consider appropriate only for a father.

Thus it is that in each social status there are blueprints which set forth customary behavior. It follows that role is not merely a matter of action, but specifically a set of expectations for action. Whenever we enter a normal social situation, we anticipate the behavior that others will exhibit. If we take a complaint to a doctor, we expect him to listen to our symptoms, make an examination, and treat the malady with appropriate seriousness. If we are met either with flippancy or the recounting of numerous deaths associated with these symptoms, we are apt to seek other sources of medical advice. Yet we do not expect the doctor to carry his bedside manner into the drawing room, and if we meet him as fellow club member we anticipate other forms of behavior; in this context we may even be amused by the recounting of clinical cases.

Thus each person has many statuses and variant roles to play, depending upon the context. He may at one and the same time be father and son, be doctor and fraternity brother, be employer and voter. Each status has its specification in role, though normally the several roles are either separated by context or are mutually congenial. In our own complex society, where persons may relate to entirely different groups in different contexts in quite divergent or mutually exclusive ways, it is possible to have a conflict of roles. Most of us have had the experience of finding ourselves embarrassed at being in the presence of several persons who have different expectations of us. The theme is a recurrent one in drawing-room comedy situations, particularly with adolescents in relation to peer group on one hand and family on the other.

Status involves a variety of institutional areas. Kinship is one important basis of status, as the examples have indicated. In primitive societies, kin-based status far outweighs any other category. In some, the appropriate behavior of every person to every other rests upon kinship. This is true of the Arunta and the Kariera of Australia, where the entire social world is divided between kin and enemy (though often kin can also be enemies); and where all kin—i.e., everybody one meets—are classified into a small number of categories (from about twenty to forty) depending upon age, sex, and criteria of relationship. By extending the notion of kinship to include broad categories (just as we classify as uncles all the brothers of our mother and our father, as well as the husbands of our mother's and father's sisters), and by developing other customary fictions regarding lines of descent and the like it is possible for these notions to extend a simple set of roles to cover all the people in the social milieu. This recurrent phenomenon—the tendency to make kinship the most important criterion for role relationship—has led anthropologists to the widespread and involved study of primitive kinship terms and to the recognition that these patterns of classification are related to various other institutional aspects of the society.

The conformity between kin terms and other aspects of social organization need not be explored here, but it is important to recognize that kinship systems are patterns of status and role, and that the use of a kin term evokes certain expectations. We are all well aware of the wider connotations in such a word as *mother,* which is expected to carry with it not only the anticipations of particular forms of behavior, but actually to evoke special emotions. The point is perhaps more readily made by reference to a common phrase in our culture: the situational context of a love-making scene is tangibly altered when a young lady rejects the advances of a suitor with the phrase "I can only be a sister to you."

The extension and classification of the role aspect of kin relationships often establishes a veritable grammar of kinship, in which categories have an internal consistency. It is difficult to convince students of anthropology, struggling to understand the involvements of the Arunta eight-section system, that far from being complex, such a system is a clear-cut, orderly arrangement that simplifies social intercourse by creating a small set of neatly defined statuses and their appropriate roles. Our own statuses are defined far more variantly, are disclosed by far subtler cues, and require a more refined adjustment in social intercourse. Kinship is a universal feature of society, and it defines certain specific and some generalized roles in all societies. But its relative importance wanes as the society grows larger and more complex.

Another general consideration in role relationship derives from age and sex. These inevitable elements in human existence are fixed upon in every community as aspects of social relationships. The expectations of men differ from those of women; of the aged from those of youth. Like all fundamentally physiological facts, these are not merely the recognition of inherent capabilities and limitations (though often based upon them), but are given special cultural meaning. In our own cultural background we have the chivalrous tradition segregating sex roles (though modern life has introduced no little confusion in these matters), whereas primitive societies have very different forms of expectations for men and women. Indeed, the terms *matriarchy* and *patriarchy* are efforts to generalize sex roles with respect to family authority, and though they are far too generalized to be of use in understanding the complexity of social relations, they do suggest the possible divergence of expectations resting upon this single criterion.

A welter of other considerations enters into establishing status in one society or another. Heritage, immediate circumstances of birth, physical qualities, residence, special talents, possessions, and occupation are all apt to serve as a basis for status distinctions.

In American society, occupation is a primary criterion of status. Such a criterion will not be important where all men essentially do the same work. But where there is division of labor, and particularly with increased specialization of jobs, occupation has come more and more to be the major determinant of status. In fact, most of our social contacts are with persons we meet in particular economic relationships: the boss, the colleague, the grocer, the delivery boy, the doctor, or the banker, and our role relationships are set by the appropriate expectations in these particular contexts. We know so many people in particular role relationships that we often forget that these persons have other attributes connected with other roles. What teacher—and this must also be true of most occupational groups in modern life—has not felt from time to time that his students see him only in that limited role relationship which his status demands and that they fail to sense the other roles he fills? We have all known a person in some particular role relationship and later discovered unsuspected involvements that could only be uncovered in some other type of association. Much of the drama of the recent TV program in which a cobbler knows opera and a jockey knows art rests on this presumption of roles appropriate to a single criterion.

If status connotes role, and role involves privilege, then it follows that status has meaning in terms of the hierarchy of values, that status has meaning for prestige and power in the community. Indeed, popular usage has diverted attention to this hierarchical use of the term *status,* and some sociologists prefer to use it only in this way. A great deal of the literature on social status, especially in modern society, rests upon this more specialized meaning of position. It has to do with class and caste.

Not every status is a matter of hierarchy, yet every society recognizes a hierarchy of statuses. We have spoken of the status and role of an uncle, which in our society connotes very little with respect to superiority in prestige or the privilege of authority. Such a status has no hierarchical (or vertical) component. Yet certain statuses are recognized as being higher than others. Such vertical difference is generally associated in America with occupation, which, as already indicated, is one of the most important role determinants in our society.

Vertical status is closely associated with the value system

in the community, and high status is usually defined in terms of values: either the special rights and the desired roles or the paraphernalia and material equipment that are the symbolic element in the value system, or both. Furthermore, high status is closely associated with authority, though the one is not entirely dependent upon the other. In simpler societies hierarchical status may be based on little more than sex and age, though even here certain offices may exist which carry special status. Among these, the most recurrent is the shaman, which is the anthropologists' term, borrowed from the Siberians, for those persons who are practitioners of magic arts for curing or killing.

In more complex systems the elaboration of values is generally accompanied by a corresponding elaboration of statuses on a hierarchical basis. It is often possible to divide the whole society into a series of social layers, the members of each sharing general hierarchical status, each ranked according to the value system prevailing in the society. Such social layers are called *classes* or *castes*. Castes are those classes which are so rigid that no person may properly move out of the one into which he was born. It usually means, for reasons that are self-evident, that he must marry within his own caste. Classes may have varying degrees of fluidity, but unless there is a sense of unity, unless they can be said to form a social group, it does not seem proper to speak of classes, except in a loose and literary way. It should be made clear that whereas hierarchical status is universal in human societies, class systems, the sharp demarcation of social units based upon such a hierarchy, are relatively infrequent. They tend not to be found at the truly primitive levels of society, but rather to appear in the more complex social systems, built upon a developed agriculture, but without industrialization in the modern sense. Class systems are to be found in what we will here call primitive state systems; i.e., early politically organized societies. Elaborate class and caste differentials were found in the Kingdom of Buganda in what is now Uganda, among the peoples of Ruanda-Urundi in the Belgian Congo, throughout much of southeastern Asia, and in the Aztec empire prior to the conquest. They are also characteristic of the ancient Mediterranean world— we forget that the democratic Greeks had classes—and in Europe prior to the Industrial Revolution.

As much difference in status may be found in a society without social classes as in one with them. The French political writer de Tocqueville remarked on the great divergence of status despite the absence of classes in America a century ago. Though many scholars have subsequently tried to show the existence of social classes here, his remarks remain true today. No one would doubt that vast differences in social status exist in America or that most people live their lives within a rather narrow status range —yet we do not have two classes.

In discussing values, a distinction was made between those which are ascribed and those which are achieved. A similar distinction can be made with respect to status (in its hierarchical meaning). Ascribed statuses are those which a person holds through circumstances beyond his own control: his sex, age, tribal or clan affiliations, or the inheritance of a title to nobility. Achieved statuses are those which he holds through actions he has himself taken. The Plains warrior who struck an enemy and the self-made captain of modern industry provide examples of achieved status. In some cultures, most significant statuses are ascribed: each person is born to a clan or a class, and there is little or nothing he can do to alter it. In others, most statuses are achieved; certainly this is true in our own. We say that anyone can be president and believe that a man is what he makes himself. Our culture has an ideal of social mobility, and persons are expected to achieve the status they have, though circumstances of birth are not entirely disregarded.

When it is possible for a person, through his own actions, to determine his position in the social hierarchy, it can be said that there is a high degree of social mobility. Where the society sets the position of each individual in terms of arbitrary, external criteria, then mobility is at a minimum. As we said, no society is completely fluid; there is none which avoids all arbitrary classification. Similarly, there are no completely rigid societies; modern studies of the Indian caste system have shown a considerable amount of social mobility even within its relatively rigid structure.

Since status involves roles, prestigeful status also involves special roles. In general, the privileges of any high status outweigh its onerous obligations and make that status desirable. Contrary cases can be cited: we have the slogan that the presidency is a killing job; the Ba-Ila, a Bantu-speaking people of Northern Rhodesia, say that chiefdom is serfdom. Despite the disadvantages that may befall a person enjoying a high prestige rating, such positions never fail to attract personnel. After all, the desire for status, the seeking after values and value symbols, is an extension of the basic desire for acquiring positive affect; it is the response to a basic motivation, carried on in the symbolic world of culture. High status is therefore a desideratum for which people regularly undergo hardships and disadvantages and in many cultures even suffer indignity and death.

AUTHORITY

Societies, however simple or complex, do not run of their own accord; the activities that make up the daily life of a people require direction. Nor do cultures continue of their own accord; attitudes and beliefs require support and reaffirmation. There must necessarily be decision making, and decision making must be allocated among the personnel of every society.

The allocation of decision making may be called the system of *authority;* the exercise of authority may be called *control.* Authority is the established right of persons to make binding decisions regarding some aspect of the life activities of others. It is the recognized right of the parent to send his child to bed, of the tax assessor to impose an excise, of the judge to sentence a culprit, of the priest to order a ritual. Systems of authority inhere in every social system, but the allocation of authority, the selection of personnel, the range of action, varies from one community to another. Control may be seen as one aspect of social role, one aspect of behavior that is expected of certain people in certain times and places. Since authority has an important part in the character of social organization, it must be given particular recognition.

It is useful to distinguish between legitimate and usurped authority. The latter is the exercise of control over others in a manner not sanctioned in the culture. The act of revolution is the usurpation of power; so also is the act of a tyrant, when that action goes beyond the established cultural usage. Anthropologists have rarely had the opportunity to study such power formations outside the normal or legitimate authority, though we do have evidence of its occurrence. Thus the Andaman Islanders vest legitimate authority in the elders, but from time to time a young man of particular qualities obtains an influence beyond that considered appropriate for his age. Among the Ba-Ila of Northern Rhodesia, the women withhold their favors from the men in protest against some act of their authority. The shaman, with his occult knowledge, sometimes acquires power, and among the Yokuts of Central California has teamed up with secular authority. By the very nature of anthropological inquiry into primitive behavior, these examples are not entirely lacking in legitimacy, for they must be recurrent and recognized patterns of behavior in order to reach the anthropologists' notebooks at all.

It is useful to distinguish three kinds of authority: (1) reinforcement, (2) administration, and (3) adjudication. *Reinforcement* is that authority which forces conformity to accepted standards of behavior. Parental control of children, priestly admonitions against sin, criminal courts punishing a murderer, are examples of reinforcing authority. Such behavior endeavors to insure continuity of established codes and to prevent such deviations from culturally prescribed behavior as might threaten the integrity of the social order. *Administration* is that aspect of authority which directs the concerted action of the social unit. The decision to shift camp or engage in a hunt, the maintenance of public works, the arrangement for religious rituals, are examples of such administrative authority. *Adjudication* is the resolution of conflict between separate members or groups as they arise within a society. The right to decide a quarrel among children or a conflict over property is an adjudicative control.

There is a popular notion that primitive peoples are ruled by custom, that their life continues on its own momentum and that primitive man blindly and undeviatingly follows the paths trodden by his fathers. Custom is the ultimate basis of all authority, but neither the primitive nor the civilized man always follows custom. Anthropological theory has to a surprising degree accepted this idea of primitive conformity to the dictates of custom, even though the ethnographic accounts of particular tribes repeatedly show that primitive deviation and conflict occur.

No analysis of social systems can possibly comprehend human behavior without an awareness of the need for, and the universal existence of, authority. Authority and custom are mutually reinforcing; authority preserves custom and custom legitimizes authority.

Authority, then, is role behavior; it is part of the systematized sets of interpersonal relationships which characterize all social life. It operates within a context. It is well to recognize that fundamentally authority lies within groups, though it may extend beyond, and that it is defined and limited by custom. Within the modern family, for example, the right and duty of the father to chastise his son is delimited by customary and legal considerations. Custom demands that the father (and in varying degrees, his wife) exercise control over a child's behavior so that it does not engage in wrongful acts; that he administer the economy of the household and allocate its resources, and that he adjudicate the disputes of his children. The nature of this authority has changed during the past century, but it still rests on custom. In this case, as regularly in modern society, it is also circumscribed by specified law: a father cannot prevent his child from going to school.

Authority is infinitely divisible by specification. For this reason, terms like *patriarchy* must be used with extreme caution because they summarize and oversimplify an extremely complex phenomenon. Similarly, the right of decision by husband over wife and vice versa, which is the subject of so much humor in America, is always limited and defined. Constellations of authority exist within primitive families and also exist beyond them. The extension of family systems of authority to comprise larger familistic units called clans is a frequent aspect of primitive patterns of control.

Adjudicative authority has been specified as one kind of recognized power, but whereas adjudicative process is

found in all societies, the power to render judicial decisions is not. In the more primitive social systems, adjudication is a matter of individual or group action, and "rests
upon the lance," as the Philippine Ifugao say, rather than
upon the authority of a decision-making functionary.

Among the Eskimo, the Ifugao, or the Yurok of northwestern California, and among innumerable other tribes,
a dispute takes the course of direct action. If a person con-
siders himself to be wronged by the action of another, he
has no recourse other than to avenge that wrong. He may
(and in clan societies he generally does) call on his family or
other group to aid him, and his assailant will do likewise.
Such adjudication has its ultimate sanction in physical
strength, but there are regular procedures for avoiding
physical combat. For instance, the Eskimo have two forms
of dueling: wrestling and the song duel. In either of these
the two principals settle the matter in direct contest before
the whole community without resort to bloodshed. The
Yurok and the Ifugao both employ elaborate bargaining
techniques to settle legal affairs, using intermediaries who
help them arrive at an agreement and who give legitimacy
to the procedure but who do not have any decision-making
power (much as we use agents in the transfer of real
estate). In all these cases, the community interest in amicable settlement is represented; it stands as a kind of informal arbiter, but it has no power to render a decision
that is binding on the parties involved. Thus the law may
be quite clear and procedural rules firmly set, while there
is no specified person of authority capable of enforcing
either. This pattern is regularly used in clan-organized
societies in disputes between clans and is also the regular
procedure for separate geographical entities, whether these
be small bands of the Australian aborigines or modern
states.

Systems of authority are associated in our minds with

the notion of government, though it is clear from the discussion thus far that the term is being used in a much broader sense here. If by government we mean the allocation of ultimate authority over the actions of individuals living within a broad territory, government is frequently wanting at the more primitive levels of social organization. Indeed, while authority patterns are universal, governments are not. The popular notion is that each tribe has a chieftain who can act for the tribe. Much harm has been done by operating within this conception: treaties have been made, lands "bought," and similar contractual arrangements have been entered into with a spokesman who was presumed to be acting for his tribe, in the manner of a governmental head, as we know it.

Perhaps the least developed organization known to anthropology is represented by the desert Shoshone Indians of Nevada and some of the Arctic Eskimos. In both instances, environment makes group life impossible for a good part of each year, so that individual families—a man, his wife or wives, and their children—or at most two or three closely related families, act independently for a good part of the year. In those cases, such families come together in temporary villages when they can sustain more concentrated populations. But the absence of any strong sense of geographical unity means that a family does not necessarily return to the same seasonal village each year. Under such circumstances, it is not surprising that there is no chief or headman with any real authority, though certain persons may be regarded and deferred to as wise and their counsel sought. Even the more populous and settled Shoshone areas have no official with any powers except a kind of leader appropriately called the Talker, for his authority goes no further than his powers of persuasion.

More often there is a clear sense of boundary. The band

of peoples who live and operate together know the limits of their territory and distinguish those persons who have a right to its use from trespassers. Such bands are found in a good part of the more primitive areas of North America, in Australia, and among such pygmy groups as the Andaman Islanders. But even here there is no chief, strictly speaking. Among the Andaman Island Negritos, the senior men—usually there are only three or four of them at any one time in a normal band of two or three dozen persons —provide such governing body as exists, making decisions binding on this small local group. Here, as in most similar circumstances, there is no larger group, no wider territory, over which a recognized authority is exerted. Each band is a separate entity; it may be at war, under truce, or enjoying friendly relations with neighboring bands, but it does not act in concert with them in formal and continuous cooperative endeavor. This absence of broad territorial control is found in societies with more advanced technologies as well. In the highlands of New Guinea, for example, each small farming village is separate and is the potential enemy of every other. The relationship between them is apt to be determined by relative strength.

Ties of kinship frequently serve to unite separate social entities of this kind. Marriages may cement alliances in primitive cultures as well as in European states, though their official relations are often a source of friction. In many societies the bonds of kinship are given special emphasis through a system of clans, i.e. groups with a strong sense of solidarity, which are unified by bonds of real or fictitious kinship, but which are not spatially delimited. Clans often serve to hold together larger geographical areas, but individual loyalties are often to the clan rather than to a geographical entity of a kind we might call a tribe. That is, authority over clan members rests with clan leaders, whereas the geographical unit has no clear authority other than that established through the local leaders of each separate clan. Secret societies, such as are found in Melanesia and in West Africa, or special organizations like the Plains Indian military societies, may act openly or surreptitiously as a governing body because they have managed to garner considerable strength and because they cut across more limited social entities.

In societies where each separate band or each separate clan is a sovereign entity, we can hardly speak of government. There is, rather, a kind of paternal control resting in the hands of the senior men. There may be peaceful coexistence among them which is frequently a kind of truce in which each recognizes the power of the other and normally avoids recourse to arms. But this is not government; it is the adjudication of disputes between separate social units, already noted.

In societies where there is no power operative over the whole system (that is, where separately controlled social units lie cheek by jowl with one another and recognize no higher authority) they may nevertheless be part of one social system if (1) they consider themselves to be such, and (2) they operate within a common set of norms for conduct, so that (3) peaceful adjudication regularly takes place among them.

Political authority or government is the unified system which provides territorial integrity through the centralization of decision-making procedures. When a general basis for such decision-making powers provides unity of administration over an extensive area, we can speak of *statehood*. Such authority systems supersede the pattern of decision making through the use of power in the form of feud (though the state itself may engage in feud with neighboring states). Indeed, the existence of a state requires that the use of force and the reaching of decisions rest entirely in its hands, except as it allocates such au-

thority to subordinate powers. For example, in the native
kingdom of Buganda (which is part of the present protec-
torate of Uganda in East Africa) the king denied the clans
the right to seek their own justice and insisted that all
disputes be adjudicated by the royal court. This is also
exemplified in the outlawing of feuds in modern America and in the establishment of special tribunals to provide
legal means of settling labor disputes without the use of
violence.

Where social systems take on the complexity of states,
they inevitably involve the hierarchical arrangement of
powers: a series of subordinates with limited authority
delegated by higher incumbents. Such systems of authority
may be called *bureaucracies,* which in turn have their own
structural requirements. In theory, authority is placed at
the apex (and in democracies, ultimately upon the elec-
torate); in practice, it is difficult to determine just where
power and control actually rests. We may put it this way:
where there are intervening levels between the ultimate
power and the final action, there is an erosion of the
authority away from its presumed location. The inability
to maintain direct supervision, the inability to know and
understand the details of operation, the intervention of
strong wills at levels that lie between the authority and the
action, all tend to deprive the former of some of its control of the latter. These problems of bureaucratic organization beset not only modern governments but also private
corporations and other large aggregates in modern life.
Similar problems may be seen at the level of primitive
states; for example, the king of Buganda took action to
prevent his local chiefs from gaining too much private
wealth and power. For this reason and for others, it is not
always possible in large organizations to determine just
who has just what powers. The situation is made more
complex in both primitive and civilized democratic systems

by the fact that ultimate authority rests in part upon public consensus and in part upon established custom—which is inherited public consensus.

Beneath any system of legitimate authority rests the culturally accepted use of punishment and reward, which may be called *sanctions*. The systems of punishment and reward vary greatly, from the physical to the psychological, and include (as punishments) ostracism, ridicule, and the appeal to supernatural power; (as rewards) the granting of privilege, status, or physical well-being. The right to evoke these sanctions is apparent in positions of authority and may be considered a measure of them, though perhaps a better measure is the degree to which a person in such a position is obeyed without recourse to sanctions. A true state involves the legitimate monopoly of power in the hands of its rulers.

Such a right may be held not only by an individual but by the community. This applies in particular to such sanctions as ridicule and prestige—which in a certain sense go hand in hand. Eskimo song duels involve mutual ridicule in front of the whole community. Ridicule is probably a universal weapon in an informal way, but occasionally it is institutionalized. Among the Ba-Ila of Northern Rhodesia, who are extremely proud and quick to take offense at an insult, a person may publicly ridicule his age-mates and the age-mates of his father. Among the North American Plains Indian tribes, a man gained prestige through exploits of war, and could recount his deeds of valor at every public occasion.

Such frank and open uses of prestige and ridicule require a rather small and intimate group. They are therefore more effective as broad instruments of power in relatively primitive communities; in a broader sense, however, some measure of public approval underlies all sanctions. Ultimately, legitimate powers rest upon consensus and evoke community feeling for their proper application.

In summary, authority is the power of decision over the life activities of others. It is an aspect of social role which has particular importance in the operation of the social unit. It is the legitimized use of force to insure conformity, unity, and harmony in the actions of a social entity based upon the established concept of correct behavior.

IDEOLOGY

Man everywhere discovers his environment through the perceptions supplied by his culture. Much of this learning is verbal, so that the language and thought create a picture of reality within which the individual operates. Through language, a kind of rationale is imposed upon the known universe, giving meaning and unity not only to nature but to the behavior of people as well. This intellectual and spiritual rationale for the *status quo*, we call the *ideology*. The ideology provides the basic metaphysical assumptions, tying the observed and observable phenomena of the natural and human environment into a kind of unity, filling in the voids of knowledge with religious and magical belief, and ultimately supplying a system of justification for the circumstances of existence.

In this presentation we are not concerned with the metaphysical or mystical aspects of religion, but with the social, i.e., with the degree to which ideological considerations and moral beliefs contribute to ordinary social intercourse. For ideology is the blueprint for action as it is perceived by the members of a society. Ideology is the system of ideas by which actions are guided and against which they are judged. Every society has such a system of assumptions and beliefs which tend to form a coherent whole. The system relates to the world of reality in terms of the society which adheres to it, and the system of beliefs itself also creates reality. For man, as we have already said, largely perceives his world through language before he experiences it, and language gives form to his perceptions.

Ideology is quintessentially culture; it is built out of past experience and belief. Our concern, however, is not particularly with belief, but rather with the part that ideas play in supporting a given social organization, for each of the components of social organization is ultimately justified in terms of the ideological system. Ask why certain values are held, why certain statuses are distinguished, or why certain roles are appropriate, and the answer will be couched in terms of a presumed orderliness in the world. Reference to a systematized understanding applies to all the components, but we can see it better with respect to authority, inasmuch as authority invokes expressed rules of conduct and is itself expressed when such rules are broken. It is in law that the ideological system which underlies social organization comes to the surface and is fully exposed.

All people have law in the broad sense of the term. Regulations govern the life activities. Tabus are laws; marital restrictions are laws; recognition of rights and privileges are laws as well. They may not be codified and are certainly not written. There may be no special vested authority other than the community as a whole to apply sanctions of force and the vaguer sanctions of ridicule and prestige. Nevertheless, they are laws in the sense that they are agreed-upon modes of behavior, the breach of which calls for such sanction as the community has the means of applying. In the final analysis, laws always rest on an ideological system, whether we are speaking of the fact that a king can do no wrong (based upon the idea of the divine right of kings or the fact that the king is the law) or whether we are exacting an eye for an eye (based upon the notion of balanced justice and appropriate punishment).

This brings us back to a point in the preceding section, the distinction between legitimate and usurped power. Legitimate power is that which is justified by the ideology; usurped is that which is not. It is a distinction hallowed in our own legal system (which developed in a period of new authority and new ideology) that the constitution provides for government by law and not by men.

The emergence of American institutions is a good example of the need for an ideology. Because this continent has been peopled by diverse groups with variant ideologies and different religious philosophies, it has been difficult to forge a unified system of belief which in turn can sanction a system of authority. Yet certain principles emerge as unassailable, as matters to be taken for granted. Among these are the sacredness of the individual's rights, where they do not infringe upon those of others; the associated right of freedom of contract; the recognition of ownership as a private relationship between individuals and things. On the other hand, these operate in a context which recognizes the primacy of national consideration and the need for subordinating individual rights in matters of public concern. General-welfare clauses are found in all modern legal systems. We see this individual subordination to the demands of the state in times of crisis: the free individual is conscripted for war and sent to his death. This is not to say that ideological differences have entirely been resolved nor that there are no breaches of conduct contrary to such rules as exist, but rather that both established law and emergent custom build upon certain general unities against which action is properly judged.

Primitive law similarly rests on an ideological base, which, though different from our own and leading to other regulations, is self-consistent. The Tlingit Indian of south-

eastern Alaska who accepts his own death in recompense
to a clan, because one of his own clansmen killed a man
of that other clan, is operating on a set of assumptions: the
subordination of the individual to clan unity, the differential valuation of individuals based upon social status, the
nobility of the sacrifice and its post-mortem reward, and
the notion of reciprocal justice are among the principles
which render the act a logical outcome of premises. Not
that this Tlingit warrior wants to die, any more than
modern soldiers want to die in battle. Nor need we believe
that every Tlingit will face such a trial with equanimity
or that none will shirk his duty. Laws everywhere are
broken, but everywhere they exist and take their shape
from an underlying ideology.

A principle of great importance underlies all ideologies
and, indeed, all of social interaction. This is what Robert
Merton has called "the self-fulfilling prophecy," but it
might better be called the self-validation of social attitudes.
This principle is that a belief generally held gives rise to
action which validates the original belief. In the fear of
magic, people die, thereby justifying the belief in magic.
In the assumption of hereditary limitations on the part of
a racial or ethnic group, society fails to provide adequate
educational facilities and the group lacks intellectual capacity, thus nourishing the belief. The principle applies
with particular importance to the values in any society
and especially to their symbolic aspect. The value of gold
rests upon a consensus that it is valuable and a consistent
action taken in terms of that consensus. The same (with
more dramatic force) applies to paper money and can be
seen all the more clearly because, from time to time, faith
in the currency has been lost and the value of the paper
reduces to its intrinsic worth—nothing.

The self-validation of social attitudes may sound like
circular reasoning, in that the fact accounts for itself, but

it is the only means by which symbols do and can operate. The meaning of a word rests not upon its sounds, but upon the community acceptance that those sounds convey that meaning. So, too, with all symbols. This is especially important for those symbols which represent the values of a society. It is also true that the validity of an ideological system is established by the fact that people believe in its verity and act in terms of those beliefs. Yet we must not forget that both values and the broader frame of reference within which those values operate—the system of belief and assumption—ultimately are rooted in the external conditions of society. They relate to the realities of life, the nature of man himself, and the circumstances under which he must fulfill his inner demands.

In the modern world, the ideological and explanatory system is increasingly scientific. Modern tools have rendered the natural world more understandable than ever before. Yet how lacking our knowledge remains and how poorly we perceive the manifold character of the real world even with such modern instruments. How much poorer this knowledge was a century ago; how infinitely poor among primitive men. For man learns from experience; he learns to see the relations between events and to calculate those within his experience that are predictable. The distinction between the scientific and the prelogical mentality cannot be sustained, for it is easy to show that primitive man reasons with accuracy, that he can read from minor clues to the greater whole. How else could the Australian native track game with refined accuracy where a European woodsman sees no clue whatever? But the relations in nature are far more complex than his limited range of experience can verify. Some three or four millennia of accumulated experience since the invention of writing still leaves us without adequate answers to fundamental questions. We must fill in, as part of our ideology, the answers to such basic questions as the nature of matter and of life; man's commitment to social living, and the human and animal capacity to forgo self-interest for some external good. These dark spots we fill in with assumptions in order to make our understanding of a piece. The dark areas are far larger among those peoples who have not had the benefit of this accumulated experience; their ideology is understandably filled with more of what we call magic and the supernatural, of more imaginings unfettered by the concrete, established relationship between events.

Thus each people faces its world and finds some rationale for its characteristics. Within that world is man himself, who must fit into the system of understanding; and that system of understanding must in turn offer a basic blueprint for his actions.

Social organization is the pattern of regularized interpersonal relations among men, the network of accepted and expected interactions among persons who constitute a society. Man, being committed to social action, must live within the context of social relationships. These social relationships are governed by the principles or components of all social systems: the formation of groups, the adherence to specialized values and their symbolic representations, the recognition of particular statuses and the appropriate roles for each, the allocation which places the control over certain persons in the hands of others, and the acceptance of general principles which afford a systematic matrix for these several kinds of action and attitudes.

The manner in which these several components are fulfilled can vary widely. In the next chapter we shall see the broad basis for the variations in man's way.

The Mechanisms
of Social Evolution

EVERY SOCIAL SYSTEM is different; every systematic explanation of social behavior must recognize the variety as well as the unity in human conduct. The major differences that exist in social systems can be explained on an evolutionary basis, and it is the purpose of this chapter to develop a theory of social evolution.

Fundamentally, an evolutionary hypothesis involves the assumption of a tendency toward growth in social systems from simple to complex. In the theory set forth here, the forces that make for growth lie in the natural tendency for the means of production to develop and improve. Social institutions do not provide the basic dynamic of evolution; in a sense, they do not themselves evolve. Rather, they adjust to meet new circumstances as they arise, either through a change in environment or through a technological growth. Of these two factors, technological growth is not only the more usual but is also the factor which contains a measure of regularity. Since technological development brings about new conditions for social interaction, and since these new conditions tend to be repetitive in their effects, a recurrence of certain general features of social organization may be expected and can be shown to occur among different societies enjoying similar technical advances. Thus it is that society has the appearance of evolving, and it is appropriate to speak of it as evolving.

This evolutionary theory is also a functional theory in the sense that it involves the basic functional thesis that (1) institutions are mechanisms of social interaction which serve the continued life of the society, and (2) all parts of the social system must form an integrated whole so that changes in one part require adjustments in others. In addition, this functional theory stresses the priority of some aspects of society over others. To translate a theme from George Orwell's *Animal Farm,* all social institutions are basic, but some are more basic than others. That is to say, some aspects of the situation have immediate, direct, and consistent influences on the total structure of society, whereas others are peripheral. We do not deny that art and economy are related, nor even that art might change the economy of a society; however, it is more likely and more frequent that the economy changes the art. Furthermore, certain areas of life activity lie closer to such external factors as environment or such internal ones as technical change and are therefore more vulnerable to their pressures.

It is important at the outset to dissociate modern evolutionary theory from some of the premises of classical evolutionary doctrine discussed in Chapter II. The first of these has to do with the concept of progress. *Progress* is a value-laden term; it assumes certain values or goals toward which movement tends. Evolution may be viewed as progressive, however, only if these goals are specifically defined as the greater complexity of technical knowledge, greater capacity to produce, and increased elaboration of the body politic in performing these ends. They do not imply any moral betterment or greater satisfaction or happiness of the population. They do involve greater complexity and a higher degree of specialization in the means of production, but not necessarily any greater increase in individual capacity or knowledge or in personal satisfaction of wants. Fundamentally, it is technology that progresses; it is man's capacity to produce that evolves.

The evolutionary thesis here propounded is not teleological. There is no assumption of an inner force or dynamic underlying human behavior that makes evolution inevitable. We no more consider that the modern two-party system was inherent in the original rules of incest than we believe that the Shakespearian sonnet inhered in the first protoplasmic ooze: evolution is not the unfolding of a predetermined course. Rather, it is the chance product, the unanticipated consequences of the working out of regular forces in nature. These natural forces are not significantly biological, but inhere in the nature of the social interaction of animals having the characteristics of the human species. Evolution is a sociocultural phenomenon and therefore must have its causes in social interaction and culturally patterned behavior. Since there is regularity in these causative forces, however, there is recurrence in social consequences: recurrence, but not inevitability. For always there are factors external to the social situation which may hamper or alter development.

Nor is social evolution to be seen as ethnocentric: it is not an evolution toward us. We cannot infer the aboriginal condition to have been in any sense the opposite to our own. This is corollary to the point about progress, for evolution does not assume (or deny) that our modern condition is superior—except, of course, in those specific goals which were held to be admissible: technological superiority, increased capacity to produce, and the means of organizing an increasingly large population.

Evolutionary theory has been under attack for more

than half a century. Yet no one doubts that there has been a progressive development of man's knowledge from the time he first took on human form to the present. The archeological record clearly demonstrates this, and no archeologist expects to find evidence that would contravene it. The ethnological evidence also supports such a notion, for, although it is unfashionable to refer to modern primitives as "Stone-age men," anthropologists agree that most hunting-gathering people now living have never previously had agriculture, writing, and the like. Even if this is true in some cases—the Siriono Indians of eastern Bolivia who now live by hunting and gathering wild foods appear formerly to have been agriculturist—it would not deny the general run of events, but would represent only a particular environmental adaptation. In short, the developmental sequence of human knowledge is generally accepted.

The objections to the evolutionary theory have largely been to its excesses and exuberances: to teleological and ethnocentric assumptions. They have in no small part been to the endeavor to develop specific evolutionary sequences based upon ethnocentric assumptions. Some feel it better to speak of development rather than evolution where the teleological and ethnocentric assumptions are omitted. If, however, there is any real difference in the words, it is that *development* denies the existence of positive forces making for evolutionary progression; it implies that the growth of society just happened. Since our thesis asserts that such forces do exist, and that they are comparable to, although not identical with, those which make for biological evolution, use of the word *evolution* is the more appropriate.

We must therefore look to the regular forces that make for this developmental change and its social concomitants. There are five basic elements in the dynamics of cultural evolution: (1) the tendency for technological growth and development through time; (2) the social consequences of such technological development; (3) the process of selection of those societies and institutions that best cope with the exigencies which these changes bring about; (4) continuity through time in cultural forms (i.e., that cultural forms emerge out of pre-existing ones); and (5) internal congruity and functional fitness of the various aspects of culture. The remainder of this chapter will spell out in greater detail these several elements.

THE EVOLUTION OF TECHNOLOGY

Man's conquest of the natural world is based upon his accumulated technical knowledge, the learned behavior which enables him to wrest a livelihood from the earth and to protect himself from the elements, from other animals, and from the varying physical conditions of his many environments. It is this technological difference between social groups that is basic to the systematic differentiation of societies. The accumulated technological knowledge which is the heritage of a particular culture is inevitably the foundation upon which that society rests, for it is the means by which its members satisfy their basic animal wants and around which the institutional devices must operate. This technology is always directly related to the environment. This is not to say that the environment creates the technology, but rather that the technology and the environmen operate upon each other, that the technology is the learned means by which man utilizes the environment to satisfy his animal wants and cultural desires.

It has been popular in recent decades to disregard environmental determinants because of previous excesses of geographical explanations. But the environmental factor in human behavior is now regaining its proper place under the far more profitable and sophisticated concept of ecology —the dynamic interrelationship between the animal and its environment (including other animals, other humans, and other societies) which limits and enforces certain forms of behavior. Under the concept of ecology, one can never speak of environment without reference to the habits of the animal, which in the human animal includes his technology.

One of the enduring questions about man is his inventiveness. We know that man invents; we know that primitive man invents; we know that men in different parts of the world have invented the same things; we know that men in different parts of the world have learned to domesticate different animals and to cultivate different plants. In short, no race, region, or time has a monopoly on creative capacity. On the other hand, human beings do not work out efficient solutions to all their problems. The capacity of the human animal to make do is remarkable. The frequency with which human beings will continue an inefficient pattern of operation rather than evolve a superior method can be illustrated from every society and every epoch. There is as much evidence for conservatism and continuity as there is for invention and change. It has taken man a very long time to arrive at the technical proficiency which he can now boast. Man has everywhere and at all times improved his condition by his own imagination; he has also continued with old practices because he has failed to conceive of ways in which his circumstances could be improved or because he rejected new methods in favor of traditional or habitual ones.

Man's capacity to create new elements in his behavior is important to evolutionary theory. It is assumed here, as generally in anthropology, that man's innate capacity does not vary from one population to another (though it does from one individual to another). Nevertheless, cultural factors are influential in this, as in every aspect of human behavior. The spirit of some cultures is manifestly inimical to creativeness; the spirit of others encourages it; in most it channelizes creative capacities to limited areas of activity. These cultural factors have varied from time to time and from place to place; they are one of the forces influencing human history. They form a set of circumstances that make for uncertain and uneven development, for they are, at least to some extent, irregular and fortuitous. But other factors, too, are at work which tend to increase human creativeness as cultural complexity increases.

The fundamental feature in evolution is technological development, which, as we have said, is progressive. We need not invoke elaborate conceptual schemes of man's increased ability to harness the powers in nature to make such an assertion. The important thing is that with the various technical developments—starting with fire, string, and the use of clubs or missiles—man has increased his capacity to produce the necessary wherewithal to sustain life. The nature of culture is such that, once a piece of knowledge is acquired, it tends to be continued through the generations. Thus an invention once made and accepted continues as a part of the culture as long as that invention is useful, i.e., normally until it is superseded by a better invention. One invention is made here, another there, and a third is made in still a different place. Once made, they pass through time and space. Technology therefore is cumulative. As each people adds to its repertoire, its capacity to sustain life increases. To be sure, arts may occasionally be lost without being superseded or without being rendered inoperative by environmental changes, but such losses must have been rare. In general, such accumulation of technological advance may be thought of as having a lineal growth curve through time.

But technological growth also has an exponential quality; that is, the rate at which growth takes place increases with each successive increment of advancement. For the products of technological development are not merely higher economic satisfactions; they include also increased capacity for further technological improvement. Let us examine the major factors that account for this.

In the first instance, most technological innovations are a recombination of existing items of knowledge, as any modern inventor knows. It is therefore mathematically inevitable that the opportunity for new techniques increases geometrically as the number of basic ideas increases arithmetically. Again, technological improvement makes possible larger aggregates of population, and the greater the population the more likely are there to be new ideas. Whether we believe that each person has equal capacity to create or that there is some sort of normal distribution curve of such ability, it follows that the more persons there are, the greater the opportunity for creativity: inventions are made in the minds of men, while a single innovation can serve millions as well as dozens. Hence technological progress makes more technological progress likely. Other factors also make for increased tempo in technical evolution, but these can be laid aside for the moment.

It is in the realm of technology that innovations are most apt to be acceptable, because of the particular character that technology has as distinct from, say, family organization or religion. The difference is this: technology is a goal-directed aspect of culture, and the aims of a technical device are directly related either to comfort or gain; the direct impact of technological results can usually be seen in terms of explicit, commonly held goals in the society. In short, despite those who insist that "what was good enough for father is good enough for me," the chances for technological innovation to prove itself are relatively good, both because its ends are relatively less subject to question and because its effects are more amenable to demonstration. We do not evaluate the virtue of a gun in terms of the person whom it may ultimately shoot.

Unlike religious and political forms, unlike differences in language and philosophy, technology has its own built-in set of values. The bow is better than the spear because it shoots straighter and farther and more frequently kills. The technology is not usually evaluated on the basis of the moral propriety of the killing; the man with the bow comes home with the game. Perhaps there is no better illustration of the inexorable quality of technological development than the fact that those rural areas where the quote about father's practices have been most frequently heard are rapidly undergoing the very changes that were the subject of this conservative rejection. Further, areas rejecting such changes are being subordinated with remarkable rapidity to those which have accepted the more efficient practices.

We view technology as the wellspring of the changes that have made for evolutionary progress. The sources of technological change may be fortuitous (as we presume was the case with many primitive inventions) or calculated (as is manifestly the case in modern industry). But the ultimate effect of any new item that adds to the potential of the society is to increase the size or strength of those societies which have this new technique.

THE SOCIAL CONSEQUENCES OF TECHNOLOGICAL EVOLUTION

Though inventions may occur without reference to ultimate advantage, they have an effect on the potentialities and limitations of life itself. Thus far, we have examined only technological evolution. Most anthropologists agree that such evolution has taken place. As we are concerned with social systems, the question is: What relation exists between technical change and social behavior? Let us consider some of the immediate concomitants of technological change:

1. Technology, through more efficient exploitation of the environment, increases the carrying capacity of the land; the population increases and larger social aggregates are in constant interaction.

2. Technological development reduces the amount of physical movement required to sustain the population. It allows for increasing sedentariness. No society is completely nomadic in the sense that it has no specified territory or limitations, and few societies are absolutely fixed in that their members remain permanently in a specific place; but there is a wide range between roaming bands and societies with cities lasting through the centuries.

3. Technological advancement increases the total goods available to the population. In part, this is the result of the increasingly sedentary character of daily life, for nomadism limits the goods that can be accumulated. But in large part, the total goods are a direct product of increased freedom from the exigencies of life, increased knowledge of means, and increased productive capacities.

4. Technological advancement fosters the division of labor and the separation of economic and social functions. All societies make some division of tasks, at least by age and sex, but increased technological development and the knowledge and skills made available by it make possible and often require the allocation of different functions to different personnel.

5. Technological development enables man to have increased amounts of social leisure, i.e., the opportunity to engage in activities that do not in and of themselves satisfy the creature needs of the population.

Technological improvement has these several influences on social life, if the environment is constant. It has these effects to the degree that the change alters the economic potentialities, whether it be the invention, say, of boiling foods (thus making grain amenable to human digestion), or the reclamation of sea water (making deserts produce abundant food).

These effects, in turn, influence the likelihood of further technological development. As has been noted, increases in population make further development more likely. The same may be said for increased sedentariness of life, for increased social leisure, for accumulation of goods, and for specialization of functions. All these contribute to the exponential curve of cultural development.

The most important point about these consequences of technological development is that they in turn have their own consequences: individually and together they require adjustments in the social system, alterations in the manner in which the components of social organization can be or must be fulfilled. This point can be made quite clearly by an extreme example. We would not expect a band of a few dozen persons, hunting game and gathering wild seeds, to have an elaborate kingship or a two-party political system; nor would we expect a modern nation to have a system of government based upon the elaboration of specified kinship roles. The one could not afford so elaborate a system even if it had need of it; the other staggers the imagination, however anarchistic our philosophy may be. Let us consider some of the general changes that may take place, while reserving for the following chapters the more detailed presentation of the course of evolutionary development.

Hunting and food-gathering societies, like all others, have specified groups. Usually these groups are united on some arbitrary kinship basis—some kind of family. Where the total population of any territorial unit numbers but a few dozen, such a basis can be sustained. When, however, it increases to several hundred, this simple device is not adequate. Frequently it is superseded by some extension of the family principle: a large group, the members of which consider themselves related by virtue of applying some selected artificial rules. These social units we call clans. Clans are to be found in all parts of the primitive world, but they are most frequent in the middle range of society which is characterized by primitive farming practices, by nomadic herding of domestic animals, or in those hunting societies where special environmental circumstances make for high populations, as on the Northwest Coast of North America. Such social units are held together internally by bonds of an essentially familistic nature; they are often held together externally by little more than a kind of armed truce or by a council of clan leaders. But when a population is to be numbered in the thousands rather than in the hundreds, then such units are inadequate for maintaining the social system and for orderly social interaction, and some other device supersedes. The clan may, and frequently does, continue. But it loses its importance in a matrix of more significant features of the social system, usually some kind of political organization.

Again, hierarchical differentiation of status exists in every society. Where the group is small and production is limited, the possibilities for elaborate systems of social differentiation are also limited, though man's ingenuity in devising invidious symbols of social distinction is indeed remarkable. They are limited in part because direct social contact makes possible a more direct personal evaluation by each member of each, partly because there are fewer goods which can symbolize differentiation and because there is less opportunity for individuals to be freed from onerous work. But with technological advances and population growth, the degree to which persons can be directly known by all others lessens and the opportunity for the differentiation in social rewards increases; there is an increasing tendency to make social distinctions on a symbolic basis. Societies which number their populations in hundreds or thousands generally have sharp class differentiation supported by elaborate legal and political devices.

Paradoxically, the effectiveness of symbolization in modern society has been undermined by the very technology itself. The possibility of mass-produced goods has reduced the meaning of such symbolic items as clothes or automobiles. The search for symbolization of social differentiation is constant; the devices (such as economically inefficient or limited edition autos) demonstrate the imagination that enters into the expression of hierarchical status.

Finally, simple societies can be governed by little more than direct personal relationships, where the defined social roles based on kinship, age, and sex have a component of authority. Even societies with a primitive form of agriculture can rest their government on the extension of the kinship pattern through the device of family unity in the clan. Frequently, however, some special group will develop: a secret society, an elaborate priesthood, or a tribal council. In the simpler systems, adjudication may take place by sanctioned means of feud, either individual or group, with some ritualized means of resolving conflict and preserving peace. As societies grow, the pressure to develop some kind of decision-making machinery is great and all large social systems do have such techniques.

These examples will suffice to show how the several components of all social systems vary with changes in the underlying technological base, and with the demands and potentialities made by varying populations.

Let us not assume however, that this is a simple, automatic, and always progressive factor. For instance, it has long been known that the kinship usage of Arctic Eskimos is very like that of the modern United States. This fact is worth examining. The Eskimos live in a situation where the vicissitudes of life make it necessary for each family to be self-sufficient. In fact, an Eskimo family may go a year or more without seeing another family. In the United States the family is also isolated but for a very different reason; the very abundance of our population, together with certain historic circumstances, has tended to de-emphasize the broader familial ties within a matrix of other social contacts. While the American family relates constantly to others, each conjugal unit lives its own life within its own quarters; its economy and its fate tend to be separate from broader social involvements. Hence very different—in a sense, opposite—forces have a similar social quality and have brought about a similar response with respect to kinship and family unity.

THE SELECTIVE PROCESS IN EVOLUTION

The third element of social evolution is the process of selective change. We might call this natural selection, in analogy with biological evolution, but the phrase is misleading inasmuch as we are dealing with social and not natural processes, and in that the phenomena are similar but not identical.

The selective process is merely an assertion that in the ordinary course of events those features of a culture which are more suited to maintaining the community will continue and those less suited will disappear when two or more alternative modes are available. The process is implicit in all functional theory, which asserts that congruent modes of behavior will tend to coincide. For instance, the late British social anthropologist S. F. Nadel shows through a comparison of four African societies that witchcraft practices and beliefs are causally related to specific anxieties and stresses that arise out of the mode of social life. Again, in northwestern California Indian societies, there is a functional relationship between the social system, in which high status may theoretically be achieved by any man through his own personal actions (as with us), and an ethical system which places upon each individual a sense of his personal responsibility for his own acts (as we tend to do). Presumably in these cases some selective force made for a change in one area to conform to the needs or the requirements in another in order to provide such congruence. The process is also implicit in the functionalist notion that institutions are instrumentalities, fulfilling certain ends, as for instance Radcliffe-Brown's thesis that Andamanese initiations convey to the neophyte the responsibilities and privileges of his new status. Such theory does not assume that the people themselves view their own society as instrumentalities and create, in some Machiavellian way, the requisite institutions, but that in the processes of time these institutions have come about and have been retained because of their satisfactory performance of these requirements.

Such theoretical assumptions have frequently been made and have with more or less certainty been verified for specific aspects of social behavior. Here, however, we are asserting that they take place in general, and that the institutional machinery comes to conform to new social conditions which have been brought about through technological development.

The selective process is most clearly indicated for items of material culture, as was implicit in our discussion of the role of technology in evolutionary development. The history of Western civilization is replete with examples, and the archeological record shows the adoption of superior techniques and the loss of inferior ones, sometimes gradual, sometimes sudden. We are currently seeing the airplane replace the train as a mode of transporting people from one place to another, and there is evidence that the days of the Pullman car, once so vital to our society, are numbered. For similar technological reasons the battleship is obsolete. The horse is now but a symbol of prestige in urban and much of rural life rather than a functional item, reminding us of earlier modes of life and preserved for the pleasure it gives (like the fireplace in houses) rather than functions performed. Our whole technological advancement has been so rapid that this kind of obsolescence is a major item in current business-operation costs. Proof of such occurrences is not easy on the primitive level. We do know that in Africa the introduction of maize largely replaced such less efficient food staples as millet and was adopted in the interior before the penetration of whites. We could all recite examples of the rejection of material benefits on the basis of sentimental, emotional, or traditional considerations and could show the false anticipations of potential benefit from new inventions; nevertheless, the process is operative in the broad sweep of human history.

Our interest lies, however, in the selective process in matters of social organization. To appreciate this we must reiterate that institutions of social life are instrumentalities, that they, too, have ends, and that some operate better than others under particular circumstances. They differ from the technical aspects of culture in that their instrumental character is not self-evident, in that they lack the built-in basis for self-evaluation. (The distinction is not so sharp as the statement above implies. Men do make rational, end-oriented choices between alternate institutional patterns.) Yet even if there is no self-conscious evaluation on the part of the culture bearers with respect to the instrumental aspects of their institutions, these end-oriented qualities do render them subject to the selective process.

It will be convenient to separate the manner in which such selection operates into two categories: the internal and the external. By internal selective process we refer to the adaptive changes and adjustments taking place within a society, the shifting of institutions that result from recognized or sensed malfunctioning. By external, we mean the processes that result from competition and warfare with other social systems.

Internal adjustments may be consciously arrived at as shifts in behavior in response to a felt need, or they may result from changing behavioral modes that are not consciously directed. The former category includes many adjustments in modern society, where the development of professional understanding of institutional behavior and the accumulated knowledge of various systems has made for some rationality in social change. The formation of the United States Constitution after the weakness of the Continental Congress and the promulgation of social legislation during the depression are peaceable examples, as are all efforts to codify the laws of various lands. Revolutions and civil wars are nonpeaceful examples of efforts to change the organization of a society where it does not meet the felt needs of a people.

Hammurabi's famous Babylonian code of laws of the eighteenth century before Christ is probably the earliest recorded effort at a reform of procedures designed to bring institutional devices up to the requirements of the society. Ikhnaton's efforts in Egypt to reform religious institutions some four centuries later was another effort, but its ultimate failure suggests that it was not requisite, however desirable it may have been. On the primitive level it is difficult to find examples because of the limitations of our data. E. Adamson Hoebel cites a case from the Cheyenne

Indians of the North American plains where conscious change was decided upon by members of the military society. It is the case of Wolf Lies Down, from whom a friend had borrowed a horse without permission (leaving a token security in the form of his bow and arrows) and kept it for a year. Wolf Lies Down put the matter before the Elk Soldier society, and the affair was settled through their good offices to the mutual satisfaction of both parties. The significant aspect of this case, as Hoebel points out, is in its conclusion, for the Chiefs declared: "Now we shall make a new rule. There shall be no more borrowing of horses without asking. If any man takes another's goods without asking, we will go over and get them back for him. More than that, if the taker tries to keep them, we will give him a whipping." It is a rare instance of the formulation of a new custom among primitive people. A redefinition of incest regulations in a Papuan village in Netherlands New Guinea was promulgated by a headman who wanted to marry a beautiful second cousin who belonged to his own clan. He not only broke down an established rule, but to cloak his act in legality, he promulgated a new law, making marriage between first cousins incestuous.

Under the impact of Western culture, native peoples occasionally alter or establish patterns to meet the new external situations. An example may be taken from the Hopi pueblo of Oraibi, where a dispute between a conservative faction and a progressive one over matters relating to modernization led to a split into two separate pueblos.

Institutional adjustments may also occur without self-conscious effort. Presumably at work here is the accumulation of small individual decisions without any anticipation of broad institutional change.

To illustrate this point it is necessary to find an example of social behavior which is sufficiently concrete, and which at the same time is made up of many separate actions so

that a change could not simply be made by decree. For this
purpose the patterns of kin terms and kin usages are ideal,
but it requires a brief recapitulation. In the discussion of
social role it was seen that all people treat certain kin in
certain ways, though each culture has its definition of appropriate role. The Trobriand Islanders accorded to the
mother's brother a role very much like that which we accord to a father, and the father stands to his son much as
we expect an uncle to behave. Now kin are always classified; in American and English usage each person normally
has but one father and many uncles, and these uncles
stand in a variety of relationships (mother's brothers,
father's brothers, mother's sister's husband, father's sister's
husband). The classification of kin is a matter of language,
but the terms used not only denote a set of people, they
connote a relationship, as we illustrated with the word
sister. In most societies such kin are addressed by the
appropriate term rather than by name—as we normally
address our parents. The pattern of terms—i.e., the classi-
ficatory system applied to relatives—varies, and these clas-
sificatory patterns are called *kinship systems.*

Studies have shown that certain kinship systems tend to
be related to special types of society. For instance, in our
society we use one term for *father* and another term (*uncle*)
both for his brothers and for our mother's brothers. This
is related to the fact that one's own close family is separated from the broader family group on either side; it is a
truly separate entity. Where, however, there is a close
association with one side or the other, as is the case in
clan-organized societies, then we frequently find a different
mode of classification. For instance, among the Crow Indians of Montana, where a man belongs to the clan of his
mother and the father belongs to an alien clan, the word
for father is used to denote a wide variety of kin who
belong to the father's clan (his brothers, his maternal uncle,

his sister's son). A man calls his mother and her sisters by the same term. The manner in which kin are classified is related to the pattern of social institutions. For instance, in matrilineal societies a person tends to view his cousins on his mother's side as brothers and sisters, while the equally close cousins on the father's side are treated as entirely separate. There is a fitness between the classification of kin—the system of words used—and the institutions of the society.

If this is the case, it should follow that where the institutions change, kin-term usages should also change. Studies have been made at different places to show that shifts in kin terms do take place under changed circumstances resulting from Europeanization, but not simply by the adoption of European patterns. As these kin usages are a part of language, they are automatic patterns, and it would be inconceivable for the society to regulate usage by fiat or for the tribal elders to order such a change. Thus, such changes must be viewed as taking place without conscious effort. Alexander Spoehr, in a detailed study of the changing kinship systems of the Creek, Cherokee, and Choctaw Indians, showed that just such changes took place during historical times. The shift from a kinship system adapted to matrilineal kin groups to one that does not make such discrimination between cousins he believes to be the product of shifting social patterns, such as the elimination of the clan as an important co-operative unit, the greater independence of the elementary family, and the increased importance of the husband-wife relationship. Other studies, made by Edward Dozier of an Eastern Pueblo group which moved in among the Hopi and adopted Hopi meanings for their own kinship words and by Mischa Titiev and Louis Faron of changes in Araucanian kin usages, show comparable adjustments in social patterns. One may, as a matter of fact, consider the tendency in modern society to drop kin terms to be an expression of the reduced importance of kin in the ordinary intercourse of daily life.

Such adaptive patterns are difficult to illustrate with other kinds of data on primitive man, but it is not hard to find examples from Western civilization. The Belgian historian Henri Pirenne in his study of medieval cities shows how the shift in political institutions resulted from the growth of commerce and the emergence of medieval cities in the eleventh century, with comparable institutional changes in all parts of Europe. One of these changes was the erosion of the power of the landed nobility and the undermining of the institutions of feudalism in favor of the establishment of a middle class based upon commerce. This in turn entailed the development of a system of governance for those who lay outside the old relation between land-lord and tenant. Some two centuries earlier, city life and merchandising having become important to European economies, the development of guilds among both merchants and craftsmen was an organizational device for the new social system, providing means of communication and mutual protection among men who had a common bond of interest in their newly developed daily occupations.

About the same time that these events occurred in Europe, some comparable activities were taking place in the New World. The Aztec empire was developing under a stong internal government, the powers of the emperor putatively resting on inherent, supernaturally endowed rights, were actually based upon a body of landed freemen. Instead of a feudal system, the loyalty of these farmer-soldiers was organized through the calpulli, which were clanlike social groups; each controlled a sector of land, and membership in each was hereditary in the paternal line. But in the development of Tenochtitlan, as the City of Mexico was anciently called, the concentration of great wealth and large populations had far-reaching influence upon the character of society. Four new classes in addition to the farmer-soldiers were emerging: a semihereditary nobility, possibly independent of the calpulli and increasingly dependent upon royal favor; a class of merchants who brought products from the hinterland to supply the urban population with necessities and enrich the life of the upper classes and the priesthood; a class of artisans, separate from the calpulli or forming separate trade calpulli (the matter is not clear), who engaged in the specialized manufacturing that was a part of the new urban life; and a class of slaves who provided the basic nonagricultural labor. Little wonder that Cortez found that laws had been codified and courts established to maintain order in a society no longer capable of basing its activities on the paternalistic authority of a clan system, or that successful merchants were incorporated into the elite of this social system.

The African kingdom of Buganda, considerably less developed, also displayed the emergence of craft groups as a necessary organizational device in supplying a national economy. Here, however, the clans themselves were often converted into guilds controlling the right to engage in certain hereditary occupations. Some of the specialized labor was supplied by artisans from neighboring tribes who entered into the economy in specialized roles.

A selective process of institutional adjustment is operative in American society. The development in American patent law, as described by Walton Hamilton, will provide an illustration later in this book. For the present, we may cite the emergence of Western water laws, which after a long struggle in California ended in the complete reversal of English common law. The basic ruling, which is still applicable in the more humid Eastern portion of the country, holds that water rights are held by those along the banks of the stream, and the early California settlers followed this ruling. The character of the California landscape, however, with its large stretches of semidesert land

and its few large streams (carrying a large volume of water from the mountains) rendered the common law uneconomical. After bitter fighting the shift was made which gave broader territorial rights to water, a shift that made possible the great agricultural enterprises of that state.

Although internal selection tends to create increased functional unity, it does not necessarily lead to a more viable total society. Both the decisions of men consciously arrived at and the kind of ouija-board development that comes unanticipated from the individual responses of many men are not in and of themselves calculated to further the social system. They are hampered by the vagaries of a pre-existing power structure and the cupidity of men; they are subjected to the myopic and fallacious assumptions to which people easily succumb. In short, wisdom does not always prevail. The brute fact of the matter is that the policing of evolutionary development ultimately rests in the external selective process: the fact that each society lives in a context of other societies which offer an immediate or potential threat to the society, against which the society must rally its forces.

The external selective process is also of two kinds: the direct subjugation or elimination of the weaker social entities by the stronger, and the reorganization of institutions in the face of such a manifest or potential threat. The elimination of societies through warfare is a recurrent phenomenon, nowhere so fully illustrated as in the advancement of Western civilization through the Americas, Australia, and parts of Africa. That similar processes took place under more primitive conditions is repeatedly shown in the archeological records. Examples are to be found outside this European development, as the Chaka conquest in southeastern Africa attests, the advancement of western Polynesian culture onto certain Melanesian islands, the Inca and Aztec conquests, and the Baganda subjugation of neighbors. In most instances, it should be noted, the people who had the weaker system were not killed off, but their social systems were destroyed or radically altered. And it is the effect on social organization that concerns us.

To be sure, few if any of these examples rest solely on matters of social institutions, for the operation of this factor involves general conflict between two or more total social systems, including not only matters of institutional arrangement but also such factors as technological superiority and environmental advantages. Some, however, significantly involve matters of social organization. The Zulu conquests were made possible by the development of a strong military organization and the efflorescence of militaristic values; the only technological development on record was the shift from the throwing to thrusting spear—hardly a creative change. Significantly, the failure to supply adequate institutional mechanisms for a widespread military conquest prevented the establishment of a large-scale social order, and a Zulu empire was never created. The Incas of Peru were aware of this problem and reorganized the social systems of conquered territories in such a way as to fit them into the basic pattern, though they changed native custom as little as possible.

On the American Great Plains, between the first contact with Europeans in the sixteenth century and the final subjugation at the close of the nineteenth, acquisition of the horse and gun and the availability of fur trade altered the circumstances of life, and the tribes of the area underwent considerable change. A detailed analysis by Frank Raymond Secoy of the military operations and organizations of various Plains Indian tribes who received one or more of these new advantages and of the tribes who fell prey to those newly endowed tribes, shows the effect of external threat on the reformulation of social institutions. For instance, when those Apache Indians who were living to the east of New Mexico shortly after the Spanish arrived first obtained the horse, they continued their horticultural operations but expanded their hunting. Once their neighbors obtained the horse, the horticultural phase of their activities became a liability and was dropped, and the Apache became fully nomadic. Similar adjustments were made in other tribes, although some which did not convert to Plains patterns were effectively subordinated to those who did. Indeed, the last three centuries of Plains Indian history afford the best example of adaptive change and the selective process. Lest we view this as merely a product of Europeanization (though strictly speaking, these activities of the plains were not Europeanization, but only the acquisition of European elements after the fashion of any other cultural diffusion), we might note the development of the League of the Iroquois. The League was a social system which bound several separate tribes into a military entente so firmly that it was just short of being a nation. In fact it was called the Five Nations. In response to this threat, other peoples developed similar quasi-political institutions. For instance, four Huron tribes (also Iroquois) formed a similar federation as a protective measure against depredations on the part of the Five Nations.

The role that particular elements of social organization play in maintaining the viability of a social system is not absent from Western civilization. We can see this in the institutionalization of anti-Semitism in Nazi Germany. Whatever the value of the institution for the growth of the Nazi party, and without regard to any moral evaluation of the behavior it engendered, it can be shown that the institution itself contributed to Germany's defeat in World War II, inasmuch as it drove into enemy territory a large block of talent that contributed to the Allies' strength and deprived Germany itself of many persons capable of developing the newer military armament.

Although the selective process in social evolution may be seen as roughly analogous to natural selection in biology, it is not exactly the same because it deals with a different order of phenomena. The first of these differences is that in culture it is possible for a society consciously to change its ways. That is to say, if a society lacks an institution, if conditions change which require new social devices, then it is possible for it to develop institutions that will meet these exigencies. This difference is due ultimately to the fact that culture is a product of human thought and learning, and that the human capacity to analyze the situation makes man capable of rearranging his own affairs to meet it. Russian awareness of Western technological superiority spurred those institutions which led to her rapidly expanding educational system; our response can be similar.

One important aspect of the process of selection is that a society will often take over that element from its neighbors which has made those neighbors a threat. This must be a major factor in the diffusion of inventions of a practical kind, and it is also to be seen in social institutions. One explanation of the spread of political organization in East Africa, as represented by the Baganda and other nations of the African lake country is built upon such a hypothesis, as is the example of the Huron federation. The human capacity to meet exigencies renders social selection different from natural, but as it does not always occur, we must not overemphasize the difference.

Sometimes one society cannot make the adjustment for material reasons. It was impossible for many native tribes in America to acquire, much less manufacture, the weapons with which to stave off the encroachment of European civilization, nor could they muster the manpower. At other times the failure is social; that is, the adjustments are not made because they were antithetical to the established mode of thought, because there was inadequate awareness of the dangers inherent in existing institutions, or because they were opposed by a powerful elite unwilling to endanger its privileged position.

The second difference between selection in social systems and in biology lies in the nature of death and extinction. It is perhaps admissible to say that a society dies, but it cannot mean the same thing as to say that an animal dies, and we have avoided using the expression.

Perhaps the demise of a society is more comparable to the extinction of a species (which presumably left progeny in the form of a more highly developed species); yet that again does not seem to be quite what is meant when we speak of a society going under. We may speak of a society disappearing when its unity is broken, either by being completely absorbed into a larger whole (as with most of the Indians of the United States in modern times), or when it is fragmented into lesser parts (as in the break-up of the Roman Empire). In either case, what happens is that one society is transformed into another. Furthermore, this transformation carries with it much continuity. Not only do the people as individuals usually survive, but much of their culture will continue. Nevertheless, the institutional apparatus undergoes selective change.

This analysis shows that in the evolution of culture, the growth is not the product of a single people. The notion that a society, if left to itself, will evolve along paths similar to other societies involves false notions of evolutionary process, for in the final analysis social development is the product of the *interaction* between societies. Evolution operates through cumulative technical development, the social consequences of such technological development, and the selective forces which make for the elimination of those systems that are inadequate to the exigencies of life, both internal and external, that a given society must face.

CONTINUITY IN SOCIAL EVOLUTION

The fourth general principle in social evolution is that the process always involves emergence from the pre-existing situation; social evolution does not proceed by saltations, and new forms always have their precursors. This is simply to say that culture has continuity. But the implications for evolution are important to realize, for it means that the new forms a social organization may take are always limited by the habit patterns set by old forms.

It might be argued that since institutional devices are created in the minds of men, they are as free as the human imagination. And that is free indeed. But the conceptions of the originators are themselves fettered by their own culturally established preoccupations; and this is the first limitation on the freedom of development. Far more important, new cultural elements, by the very fact of their being *cultural* elements, must be accepted by the population in general; that is, they normally must fit the general habit patterns and expectations of the population. Continuity of culture is a standard feature of human history; it hardly needs elaboration here. Much of the older anthropology was devoted to the study of cultural survivals from past eras; it is the principal assumption of the historical schools. But our concern here is not with tracing cultural elements back through time. It is, rather, with the effect of the principle of continuity on the character and course of social evolution.

Fundamentally, continuity is the principle of cultural conservatism. This means that when circumstances require new institutional forms in a society, those forms will normally be shaped by pre-existing institutions. It may also mean that the conservative forces in society prevent institutional adaptation, often with dire consequences to the position of that society in the community of societies of which it is a part. Let us examine briefly these two factors as they influence the character of social evolution.

In the discussion of state universities, we exemplified the general principle of continuity in illustrating the historical approach. While the functional requisite of public support for education makes the institution an imperative for a modern industrial society, many features of the older patterns more fitting to an earlier society are still to be found. A student of social institutions would know, even in the absence of historical data, that the university system survived from an earlier stage of society.

Institutions not only recur in various parts of the world (which can be accounted for by social requirements); they also take on similar forms. We believe this to be a product, in part, of cultural continuity. We will illustrate this point with a discussion of clans and the varieties of clanlike institutions that are found in various parts of the world. To do this requires some digression.

We use the word *clan* in the older, generic sense, to mean a large segment of a society (a group), whose unity derives from arbitrary definitions of kinship. In this sense, true clans are exogamous (marriage between clan members would be incestuous) and unilinear, i.e., calculating membership either from father to child or from mother to child within any single system. In formal terms, the clan is a large, named, unilinear, exogamic kin group, not limited to any one location but extending the sentiments of familial ties to persons over a wide area. Usually these ties are given expression through a name or a symbol, and often their unity is re-enforced by religious sentiments, beliefs in a common ancestor or ancestral spirits, or special clan religious practices.

This kind of unity, as shall subsequently be shown, is an effective instrument for social action in societies standing somewhere between the most primitive and the more advanced social systems; they are characteristic of what is sometimes called the middle range of societies. Clans that follow this definition are prevalent in the native cultures of Africa, Melanesia, and a large part of America. They are sometimes patrilineal and somteimes matrilineal, and may vary in other details. They are highly similar in general construction however, but are so widely dispersed that it is difficult to believe they all have a singular historic source. The problem therefore arises: why the consistency in pattern? It is a problem that has been central to a great deal of anthropological theory.

To some extent this consistency derives from functional usefulness, but not entirely so, as we shall show in a moment. In part it derives, we believe, from the pre-existing circumstances. If we assume that clans develop when a society, through technological advancement, grows larger and more stable, we must place these pre-existing conditions as those out of which such growth emerged. Two elements are generally characteristic of these more primitive conditions. The first is a general orientation to family sentiments, more narrowly described than clans because they are limited to actual, traceable kin. Coupled with this is the institution of band or local group, and this tends to be unilateral, that is, to be made up entirely of men and married-in women, or (less frequently) vice versa. The clan, we feel, is built upon these institutions.

There are a number of situations where clanlike institutions occur, but where they do not take the classic unilinear, exogamous form. These, we believe, are the result of a cultural development where the social system becomes more primitive, having derived from a more advanced society but existing under circumstances that no longer can sustain the more developed institutions. One such case is provided by pioneer America. We all know the clanlike character of the Martins and the Coys, and the general pattern of extended family feuding in the mountain regions of Kentucky and Tennessee. James West, who made a study of a community in the Ozarks, indicates a tendency to form clans, but they do not have the classic structure—they are really extended families rather loosely defined.

A second instance of clanlike structures is found widely among the nomadic herding peoples of Asia and North Africa. They do not share the characteristic features of clans in the sense we are using. In part this is because herding requires a different structure; but it is significant that this herding mode of life derives from a more developed civilization. This situation will be more fully described later. A third instance is supplied by Polynesia. The family unit of the Maori of New Zealand and in much of that island world has many clanlike characteristics, but it lacks unilinear descent, and thus does not have the true clan structure. We believe that this is because Polynesian culture derived ultimately from a more developed social system and adapted itself to the more primitive circumstances of island life. There is a good deal of evidence for this in Polynesian culture, though it is by no means universally accepted by specialists.

These instances suggest that clans and clanlike social units are a natural solution to the organizational problems at the middle levels of society, so that they tend to appear no matter what the historic background was. But they also suggest that the characteristic form of the unilineal exogamic familistic group has its sources in a common pre-existing condition.

The manner in which the aboriginal transfer from band organization to family organization might have repeatedly taken place is illustrated by the native social organization of the many tribes of central California. Many of these tribes show an intermediate step, a pattern reaching toward but never quite realizing the full potentials of the clan system. In some California tribes these extended family units had names; in some they had special rites of intensification; in some they had totemic beliefs; in some they extended the bonds of kinship fictitiously beyond those that actually could be traced. All these features never appeared in any one society; it was as if the social organization was caught in an intermediate position, waiting for some final circumstance or personal act to fulfill the potentials of this mode of organizing social life.

Cultural continuity can play a negative role in evolution. The inertia of custom may prevent a society from making the necessary institutional adjustments and prevent it from developing the potentials for advancement. The point applies to the acceptance of new technologies, as well as to new institutions. The history of statecraft in Europe, especially in Germany and Italy, exemplifies the early failure to make the institutional advances which would enable the area to take maximum advantage of the potentials of the newer technologies, and many feel that European political organization is still hampered by old loyalties and institutional devices which prevent a necessary unification.

These conservative forces are responsible for a feature that seems to characterize the process of social evolution; namely, that further advances are generally not made by the most advanced society in an area, but by some of their neighbors. Patterns of life become crystallized in the advanced group, preventing a breakthrough to further development, while a people who have less vested interest in established patterns may have the requisite flexibility. The point can be most easily illustrated by the history of the alphabet. This crucial device of modern civilization evolved through several successive stages, each new stage contributed by a people who learned the notion from the preceding group, but who were not tied by habituation to the older form, though in some cases they built upon it. The same principle, it seems to us, accounts for the fact that the advance in civilization throughout the ancient world was accomplished by successive peoples, rather than by the continued advancement of a particular group. The same rise and decline (which has been the subject of no little amount of philosophical speculation) applies to the modern world.

Conservatism in culture tends to create a principle of continuity which has one or both of two effects on the course of social evolution: to stamp successive institutions with the patterns of earlier forms of behavior, and to make it more likely for cultural advances to take place through successive contributions of separate societies, rather than as the product of a single community.

CONGRUITY IN CULTURAL PATTERNING

Closely associated with temporal continuity is institutional congruity, or internal harmony in social forms (yet to some extent they have opposite effects). By this we mean that any social system requires a minimal kind of harmony among its parts, and changes will take place so as to increase the internal consistency of its institutions, where the development is not hampered by conservative tendencies. This idea is what Ruth Benedict has called cultural patterning, and what is now generally accepted by anthropologists under varying concepts such as themes or ethos on one hand or equilibrium on the other. Here we are not concerned with the niceties of the distinctions that have been developed, but rather with the general influence on social evolution.

The need for congruity exists both on the psychological and the social levels. Forms of child conditioning will carry their effects into various areas of life, and the individual will tend to see his world with a measure of consistency that his induced temperament demands. On the social level a certain uniformity in expectations and a meshing of parts will make for a more orderly social life and hence for a better functioning social entity.

Benedict's central thesis that an over-all pattern of behavior inspires the participants of any one culture is illustrated with examples from the Southwest, the Great Plains, the Northwest Coast, and Melanesia. She shows how attitudes and actions are consistent between various spheres of social life in each case.

Perhaps the process of patterning can best be illustrated by an example of changes in our own society. A major change has taken place in the role of the father vis-à-vis his sons in American society, from one of stern and remote disciplinarian to what is sometimes called the buddy-type father, who may still mete out punishment but is expected to be warm and close to his sons. (It would be hard to think of a nineteenth-century teen-ager calling his companion by a kin term carrying the connotation of father, but the contemporary slang *daddy-o* now fits the implications of the kin term from which it derives.) Contemporary with this change have come a number of other shifts in the relation between senior authority figures and junior males. The most obvious is the relation between boss and worker, where the employer is expected to be understanding and helpful rather than the remote arbiter and decision-maker. We can point to similar shifts in banking, among the clergy, and in educational and penal institutions. It is not our task here to analyze the ultimate cause for this development, but only to point out that there is a consistency in the shift, providing a new congruity insofar as the change has been completed.

Another example, more concerned with matters of organization than attitude, is the recurrent tendency to set up each formal group in our society with a constitution, by-laws, and a uniform set of officers, broadly patterned after our national government.

Recognition of this tendency toward institutional congruity does not deny the existence of the contrary tendencies toward change. These we have noted at length since they are the factors which make social evolution possible.

The importance of congruity in evolution lies in the fact that it accounts for the reformulation of the total social system after the introduction of new elements. Thus a society in which some external circumstance has brought about a major change will tend to bring its total institutional system into conformity with the demands of such a change. A shift takes place in the external environment in a society, requiring major alterations in some basic feature of organization, and other institutional aspects are gradually brought into conformity with this.

The point has already been illustrated in another context, in the discussion of kinship system changes. It will be remembered that the classification of kin and the terms used in addressing them were altered, as a result of European contact, from a pattern associated with clan group co-operation to one that fits the modern practice of individual wage work and the increased importance and independence of the primary biological family.

History also provides us with examples. It is the thesis of both R. H. Tawney, in his *Religion and the Rise of Capitalism,* and of Max Weber, in his *The Protestant Ethic and the Spirit of Capitalism,* that the development of Protestantism in its various forms was a movement which brought intellectual attitudes into conformity with the newly emergent social organization. The new order was based upon new sources of wealth made available by trade, the exploitation of distant lands, and new technologies. It required new institutions and new values and made possible kinds of public influence that were foreign to the essentially agrarian feudalism of the earlier period. Catholic philosophy did not offer an adequate ideological support for this new mode of social life, with the result that a new basic philosophical orientation began to flourish.

The argument among scholars as to whether the new ideologies caused changes in the social structure or the other way about seems fruitless; the point is that there is a requisite congruence. To us, the basic source of change is to be found in new technologies, particularly those relating to navigation, warfare, printing, and mechanics, which made a new social system possible. Indeed, the technological changes that ushered in the modern era in Europe were profound and rapid evolutionary changes which made the new institutional patterns requisite. The history of postmedieval Europe is the history of societies seeking the necessary institutional machinery for survival and growth under these revolutionary circumstances. Some, like Spain and Portugal, despite their early advantages (or perhaps because of them) never found a viable solution while others managed at least a minimal adjustment.

Our present-day world is racked with similar efforts at institutional congruency. Modern industrial production and rapid transportation and communication systems render both possible and efficient the organization of large-scale enterprises, in which fiscal and managerial ties replace kin and space as the bases for unity. This has made necessary the formation of large social units engaged in a common enterprise, with established lines of authority and decision making, unity of purpose, and a sense of community—all without ideological supports, tradition, or reenforcement through direct contact. Bureaucracy is not a product merely of government; modern business is bureaucratized, and the bureaucratic tendencies are clear in such institutions as schools and churches as well. The late Elton Mayo of the Harvard School of Business voiced a philosophy of this new social order when he suggested that corporate loyalty replace older ties; but what ideological supports ultimately will satisfy the emerging social order is far from clear.

The principle of congruity is necessary to an understanding of the character of social evolution. It is, of course, the basic principle of any theory that recognizes the internal harmony of institutions, whether it be Malinowskian functionalism, Benedictian patterning, or the sociological concept of equilibrium. Without the force toward conformity, social evolution would not take place, for we would presumably still be operating with the institutional devices of paleolithic cultures. It is the principle of congruity that brings institutions into consistency with the basic economic potentials and renders them internally harmonious.

A theory of evolution requires an understanding of the mechanism by which orderly change may take place. In the present chapter factors which bring about the progressive development of human social systems are presented under five general principles: (1) the tendency for technology progressively to develop; (2) the social consequences of this technical growth; (3) the selective process in social institutions; (4) the principle in culture of continuity; and (5) the principle of congruity in social systems. This may be called a naturalistic theory of evolution, non-teleological in character. It does not assert a unity in evolutionary sequence; it does not assume an inevitability in development. Rather, it sees the essential processes of human interaction operating in such a way as to produce long-run progressive evolution.

The forces at work in social evolution are neither immediate nor constant. Situations may arise and have demonstrably arisen in which societies remained relatively stable over millennia. Egypt is the classic example. A modern photographer can catch scenes in Egyptian villages identical to ones depicted on archeological remains several millennia old. Other examples are numerous. Eskimo life appears to be at least a thousand years old, and some of its elements go back to the upper paleolithic. The pygmies in Africa and in southeast Asia have a fundamentally similar culture and some scholars believe it dates back to the third glaciation of the Pleistocene epoch. If such continuity did not exist, there would be no modern societies close to the earlier forms of society. The processes of evolution are not necessarily gradual, nor are they fortuitous. They partake of statistical probability. Changes cannot be predicted for any given time or place; they are operative "in the long run." Circumstances may arise when a people forced into an environment lacking essential ingredients for more advanced forms (as, for example, into the Pacific Islands, the American Plains, or the South American jungles) must adjust their institutions downward, to re-create a social organization of an essentially simpler kind. On the other hand, the rapid alteration by processes of diffusion may short-cut intervening stages in any one society or cultural area.

For this reason, the presumptions of classic evolutionary theory of teleological growth—inevitability and recurrent stages, as well as their ethnocentric attitudes—must be set aside. Rather, we have tried to show that institutions are instrumentalities serving the ends of social survival, and that different institutions can serve the same ends; hence evolution is not everywhere the same. Yet the functional demands of any one situation tend to call forth similar solutions, so that recurrence is likely. We have also tried to show that change is not inevitable, so that cultures will not necessarily advance, and that advancement will tend to take place in the context of rival societies where change is forced upon a society, rather than in remote or protected areas where it is not. (The above examples of long cultural continuity are from areas that are well protected from outside influence and domination.) What we can say regarding social evolution is this: if social organization and its component elements are seen as instrumentalities, and if some serve the community better than others in a given general economic and environmental context, and if the processes of selection are operative, then it follows that the general course of evolution will have similar contours, that the more efficient institutions will tend to recur and to survive until such time as the context itself is altered.

The evolutionary explanation in this chapter presents a theory for the gradual growth and complexity of the social systems. It is built upon the data of archeology and ethnology and serves to account for the major categories and central characteristics of the known social systems. It does not in and of itself explain these social systems, in the sense that it offers a full account of what makes them as they are. Many factors, some fortuitous perhaps, some environmental, some historical, some psychological, and some perhaps even physiological, are required to explain the characteristics of any given society as it appears at a particular time and place. Evolutionary theory, like its counterpart in biology, merely offers a significant taxonomy and a general set of relationships among social systems. It is only a part of the explanatory system necessary to the understanding of why particular cultures are as they are; its important function is to provide a rough blueprint of the course of human history, the general outlines of man's way.

Evolution and the Social Imperatives

THE EVOLUTION OF TECHNOLOGY

THE SOCIAL IMPERATIVES are those elements necessary to the organization of every society. But the manner in which they are met varies from one culture to another. In this chapter we shall see that in a very general way there are regularities in this variation which relate to the economic character of the community.

The forces of social evolution were outlined in the preceding chapter and stress was placed upon the dynamic part played by technological competence in that development. Not only does such practical knowlege tend to grow, and to grow at an accelerating speed, but it carries with it implications for other aspects of culture, in particular elements relating to wealth, to the possibility for leading a sedentary life, for accumulating goods, and for the freeing of man from the daily and universal responsibility for satisfying his fundamental, animal wants.

V. Gordon Childe, in his many writings, has emphasized the importance of the invention of agriculture in the history of man and has pointed to the revolution that this invention made in man's life ways. The development of agriculture, he holds, is comparable in scope to the industrial revolution of modern times. Childe has demonstrated the rapid advance of new life ways when farming took over, and the spread of these new modes of life through the Old World, which was his area of special interest.

It is true that certain inventions and discoveries must have been crucial to human evolution, and few could have been more important than the development of husbandry, whereby man no longer lived off nature but began to create his food by sowing seeds and by protecting and nurturing animals. But this was not the only important technical advance between the time man began to control fire and that much later date when he began to harness steam. It is important to realize that technological development is wrought more by the incremental advancement of myriad small inventions than by the sudden acceptance of great discoveries. Long before the development of agriculture, as Childe was fully aware, there were numerous technical advances which progressively altered the potential condition of man. Certainly the use of chipped stone and hafting increased man's control over nature and his opportunity for survival; certainly the bow (and in the forests, the blow-gun) offered a vast improvement over the spear. The control of fire has already been mentioned, but in its simplest form this meant only that man could husband it for heat and light and perhaps reproduce it by one of the several ancient devices known to primitive peoples. Fire could roast his food, but boiling was another matter, for it required some kind of vessel; and boiling made possible the use of seeds which otherwise were not acceptable to the human digestive tract.

More particular inventions relating to more particular environments may also be noted. In central California, the staff of life was made of oak, for acorns served as the basic staple. Most varieties of acorn contain tannic acid and are either poisonous or inedible, so that the use of this com-

modity required knowledge of leaching. Without proper
techniques, and they are fairly involved, aboriginal California would have been much less densely settled. Knowledge of the use of acorns in oak-forest areas made possible
a mode of economy that could raise a hunting and food-
gathering people to a relatively high level of population
density and economic security, without any farming whatsoever.

It is neither necessary nor possible here to set forth all
man's accomplishments prior to the advent of agriculture.
The point is clear: technological advance consists of many
elements. Some are more important than others because
they have more far-reaching consequences for other aspects
of life or because they can be further built upon for future
development. We can differentiate into two broad categories the techniques of a people who merely hunt wild
animals, gather the natural products of forest and field,
who fish, collect shell fish, and the like. Among contemporary primitive peoples a great many live by the chase and
must move about from season to season in search of food.
Others, by virtue of technical knowledge and more salu-
brious environments can settle in villages. Such people are
known from contemporary accounts to have been dwelling
only on the West Coast of North America in an area extending from southeastern Alaska to central California. There
is clear evidence, however, that hunters and food-gatherers
with these more advanced techniques were not always geographically so limited. The development of a similar level
of efficiency prior to the advent of agriculture was found,
for instance, in the Eastern Woodlands region of the United
States. Evidence also exists that in the cultures of Europe
during the paleolithic, and particularly in the mesolithic
period, people had a settled mode of life without agriculture. Areas capable of supporting relatively advanced hunters and food-gatherers, however, are particularly attractive

to agriculturalists so that, if agricultural techniques are
sufficiently advanced, these areas will be taken over by
farming, because the local population itself either takes
to agriculture or will be driven out by the economically
more efficient farming peoples.

The development of farming must not be thought of as
a single, sudden change. A wide variety of possible foods
can be cultivated, and there are various efficient patterns
of cultivation. The list of plants grown must gradually have
expanded. The technology of food production involved
numerous discoveries as well. Primitive farmers cultivate
with a hoe or with a pointed digging stick. These farmers
cleared a patch of brush or forest, burned the dried bush
where it fell, and planted on the soil thus fertilized by the
ashes. This is variantly called *milpa* (the Nahuatl word for
a plot so created), *swidden* (the Scandinavian term for the
same), or *slash-and-burn*. Plots so cleared can be used only
for two or three years, then they become infertile and must
be allowed to return to bush, to be developed again in the
same way after a number of years. Such farming methods
are found in the back areas of Southeast Asia and on the
Oceanic islands, in most of native Africa, and formerly in
much of native North America. Anthropologists usually
call it *horticulture* to distinguish it from plow farming.

Several important technical improvements supple-
mented this mode of life, of which the most important are
irrigation, the use of the plow (which requires draft animals), the use of fertilizers, and the rotation of crops. All
these have the effect of increasing the caloric output in
food in relation to the caloric investment in the form of
human energy; that is, they make possible a larger or a
richer population, or both.

Where and when these discoveries were made does not
concern us here, though it may be pointed out that there
is every reason to believe that the horticultural practices

antedate the agricultural developments, and that these latter, in various combinations, have been made in different times and places. The *chinampas* of Mexico (the floating gardens of modern times), the rice paddies of Southeast Asia, and the irrigation along the Nile and Tigris-Euphrates are each so different in form and content as to make this conclusion all but inevitable.

We are all currently witness to a new set of developments and are fully aware of the gradual character of the changes taking place today. The harnessing of power in the movement of air, in the flow of water, and in the combustion of coal and other fuels (and now of course in the fission and fusion of atoms) has provided an entirely new level of opportunity. We probably see this change as sudden, but its roots go back well into the past and the ultimate implications have not yet been fully realized. It is not necessary to go into detail regarding the newer technology, but it is useful to see these changes in the light of evolutionary development, for our current experience can give us some information on the processes of evolution and perhaps an evolutionary understanding can in turn help us to understand modern events.

One further point needs to be made. Technology is an influence upon the potentialities of social existence, but it is not the only influence. Every society exists in a physical environment, and the conditions of life are always a product of the interplay between man and his environment. Since technology has effects largely because it alters the size and condition of the population, its influence is limited by the potential productivity of the environment, under the conditions of that technology. Thus we find peoples engaging in horticulture in areas so poor that their life circumstances are inferior to those of hunters and food-gatherers who enjoy a richer natural resource. Some scholars believe that primitive horticulture made no progress in

California because it was an inadequate improvement, fundamentally lacking in advantage, over the existing acorn economy. Similarly there is evidence in the eastern portion of the United States that the full development of horticulture was long delayed in prehistoric times because of the adequacy of the existing gathering economy (also involving acorns) of the peoples in that area—especially in contrast to the primitive horticulture available as an alternative. Many of the peoples in the southwestern United States, such as the Piman and Yuman tribes, practiced horticulture, but their economy was no richer than that of the hunting and food-gathering peoples of California, with their acorns, and far poorer than that of the peoples of the Northwest Coast with their salmon streams and their abundant native plant and animal life. Again, the growing of plantains is limited to certain tropical conditions, but wherever it is possible, they can sustain populations more richly than many an economy based upon the plow and fertilization. Our generalizations cannot take account of all the variations which must have occurred throughout human history, nor can we let exceptions blind us to the regularities which may be found.

With these general points on technological evolution in mind, it is possible to examine the variant manner in which the social imperatives are met under differing economic circumstances.

EVOLUTIONARY CHANGE IN GROUPS

Groups are best characterized in terms of the basis for membership. Membership can rest upon residence, upon kinship, or upon some common interests of a particular kind. The first we will call spatial, the second familistic, the third special interest.

Among the most primitive peoples in the world we usually find only two spatial groupings, the band and the tribe, and these tend to have considerable uniformity in their character. The *band* is a group which shares a common territory and exploits it as a unit. Its members defend it against trespass to protect their resources. Normally they spend most of the year together, wandering through their territory in search of food and using their knowledge of the variant possibilities and difficulties as the seasons progress. When they split up into small units, they do so out of economic necessity, and they come together again when conditions permit. The fate of the members is closely tied to the group. Furthermore, an individual normally lives his full life within the group, except that persons from different groups may marry, a fact which requires one partner to move into the territory of the other. Usually it is the wife who comes to her husband's band. This setup is called *patrilocal,* or more properly, *virilocal residence.* This places an emphasis upon the paternal line, which may be further emphasized by a rule that all men must marry outside their band. Under such circumstances the band forms a kind of lineage and may be considered familistic in the sense that the band members consider themselves to be somewhat of a kin group. Fundamentally, however, it is a residence group, for normally the wives represent a wide source of alternate bands.

Everywhere under these primitive circumstances there is a larger social entity which is generally called a *tribe*. It is normally made up of a number of bands; it usually has a name; it has a clearly delimited territory; and usually its members feel that they share certain distinctive features of culture and language. But under the most primitive circumstances, the tribe is not an action unit; it is, so to speak, only a sentiment. The members of the tribe do not get together, for instance; they have no means of organizing for common action; they have no common governance. An Andaman Islander will say that he belongs to a certain band which is part of a certain tribe, and he can give you the boundaries of each. But you may also discover that his band is at war with another belonging to the same tribe and in this fight is allied with a third band that belongs to an alien tribe. Yet the Andamanese tribal sentiment exists.

These two spatial groupings persist throughout much of human history and in pretty much the same way. Under more advanced conditions, the band turns into a village, or perhaps even a town; but these villages tend to be autonomous. The Indians of central California were organized into autonomous villages, sometimes called *tribelets,* which recognized themselves as part of a large group having a common culture and dialect. Because they were more closely spaced, several would sometimes come together under a common leader, but again not as a tribe, not with that consciousness of nationhood which we assume in modern life. The same may be said for the still richer peoples farther north on the coasts of Canada and Alaska, and for most of the peoples whose economy is based upon horticulture. At this level other groupings tend to provide a means for unifying action and giving a greater degree of social cohesion to the tribe as a whole. Yet the tribe rarely takes on a truly political character.

Some horticultural peoples hold a wider area together through weakly established political ties. This is particularly true in parts of Africa and Middle America, even where farming techniques are not advanced. With the development of agriculture the possibility of nationhood is increased, and larger political entities are held together through the concentration of power. The village entity continues, and most peasants retain their ties to the local community. Under such circumstances intermediate levels of spatial groupings—counties or regions—may emerge.

Where cities exist, wards or neighborhoods may appear and serve those who live in close proximity with mutual ties.

In broad outline, spatial groups have tended to spread outward; yet the core of a local group sharing a territory remains constant through most of human history. This core has been somewhat undermined by modern means of transportation, particularly the automobile. Larger unified geographical units that capture some of man's loyalties, and which we call states, were a relatively late development, impeded perhaps by a generic xenophobia—which is the reverse side of ties to the familiar.

At the most primitive level, family groups tend to be small units, comprising a man and wife and their unmarried children. Polygyny is generally allowed but rarely prevalent. This family unit shares a common hearth, and its adult members have their appointed tasks by means of which each contributes to the common welfare. This household—if it can be so called in the absence of houses—is the regular commensal group; it is in a sense independent of all other groups, yet it is closely tied through the band to other co-ordinate groups. At this level there is rarely any extension of such family unity, except where, as noted, the band takes on a kind of familistic quality. Among certain Australians, elaborate ties of kinship set up a series of kin groupings, though the kind and degree of their unity of action is far from clear. Clans are occasionally found.

It is with further technological development that the clan begins to assume a place of importance in the group life of primitive peoples, often dominating it at the expense of spatial unity. The clan builds its loyalty on the sentiment of kinship, drawing its members widely from within the tribe, and creating a unity by arbitrary rules of descent. A true clan is exogamous, so that it inevitably splits the family (or hearth group); each spouse is a member of a different clan and the children are all members of one or the other, according to the rule of descent that prevails.

The role of clans in the system of authority will appear later. Here, however, we must note that among many peoples the clan sentiments dominate every action. The clan becomes a kind of corporation—or corporate group, as it is called in current anthropological literature—continuing as an entity through time, holding land and other privileges, and having an internal structure providing for unity of action. The spiritual unity of each member with his clan is so great that the clan is responsible for the acts of the individual, and the individual is responsible for the acts of the clan.

In such more developed systems, the family or hearth group generally continues. The process of procreation involves two persons, and each child must be nurtured close to the woman at least. Often, however, clan loyalties are so strong that a child must live with his clan rather than with his parents, and in matrilineal societies he may therefore go to live with his mother's brother (to whose clan he belongs) rather than with his father.

Where clans dominate the organizational machinery of society, there may be groupings of clans into larger entities (which are called *phratries)* and subdivisions of them into *lineages,* or localized units within the clan. The variations on the theme are legion, so that scholars argue over definitions, inclusions, and borderline cases. But the central notion of a large group based on the arbitrary and artificial extension of kin sentiments, having economic and social functions, and unified by common ceremonies and by common religious and other symbols, is widely recurrent in that middle range of social systems which lies between the hunters and food-gatherers on one hand, and the developed political states on the other.

Where statehood enters, the clan withers, for reasons that will emerge later. Clans may continue to exist and demand loyalties, as in the relatively impotent social entities that continued in China, until recent years at least. They may take on new functions, as they had tended to in the kingdom of Buganda before European penetration. Or they may be transformed into wards or *barrios,* as some Aztec scholars believe happened to the calpulli, the twenty patrilineal geographical divisions.

Nor do we find industrial society maintaining the extended kinship ties for the organization of social life, though in modern Japan old feudal patterns retain some force and are woven into the modern industrial system. Under these conditions the family of parents and children regain importance, though the emphasis may be either on the line of descent (as is usually the case among peasants), or on the marital couple and their immature children, as it is with us.

The general evolutionary trend of kin-based group life involves the generic difference between the immediate family or hearth group and those special groups built outward into larger social units. The former are always present. They are more important under both the most primitive conditions of life and the most advanced, tending to be submerged only in the middle range of social development. The latter are absent or relatively unimportant at the primitive level, rise to frequent dominance in the middle range, decline in importance under primitive political states, and disappear entirely under conditions of industrial production.

Special-interest groups are rare at the most primitive levels of social existence. Occasionally a group of initiated men will be distinguished and form a kind of secret association, which cuts across both kin and geographical ties.

Some Australian tribes have totemic groups, made up of people whose spirits come from the same body of mythical ancestors (not a matter of paternity or maternity, but dependent upon a determination of what spirit entered the womb to bring about conception). Such units are rare.

In the middle range non-kin groups are increasingly important. Among the Indians of central California, there was a relatively weak secret society of men; on the Northwest Coast it was stronger, and such special associations were widely present in the horticultural communities of Melanesia, Africa, and North America. There is always a magico-religious aspect to such groups. They are characterized by ritual induction or initiations, by secret rites and ceremonies, and by a system of mythological justification. Often they also have a power function, uniting the senior men, the adults, or some specially selected group as against the women and children or all outsiders. Occasionally there are countervailing women's organizations. Such specially segregated sexual groups appear at the most primitive levels, but they seem to be more virulent at the more advanced, and it would be worth examining the degree to which they are associated with increased feminine power resulting from the predominantly female economic functions that develop under horticultural circumstances.

Special-interest groups continue through the remainder of social evolution, increasing in importance as the specialization of labor differentiates the life activities of various segments of the society. State systems generally have some form of guilds for each major occupation. There is almost always a special priesthood and often a ruling group. Under such economic conditions, those with the highest status are frequently a group apart, a point to which we shall turn when we discuss the subject of status.

The evolution of special-interest groups involves a gradual increase from virtual absence at the most primitive level to a great proliferation in industrial society. The earlier groupings are based largely on religious belief and separate out a body of males. At the advanced end of the scale, groups are concerned chiefly with occupation and with social and economic cooperation.

EVOLUTIONARY CHANGE IN VALUES

Lying close to the level of bare subsistence, the more primitive peoples tend to emphasize those values which are involved in the basic economic pursuits. For men (concerning which we know far more than the women), these involve the closely related skills of hunting and warfare. Strength, stamina, perseverance, and self-control are generally given emphasis. Skilled knowledge, whether practical or magical, which is believed to be of aid in the hunt is also emphasized. Industriousness may be viewed as a virtue, as for instance among the Achomawi Indians of California and the Andaman Islanders. Emphasis is also placed on maturity, and the old men are usually accorded respect —at least as long as they can fulfill the demands of the tasks that they must perform.

The community at this level is small, and a person lives his life within a narrow and clearly demarked social sphere. Under the circumstances, it is not possible, so to speak, for a person to interpose between himself and the public a symbol system and hide behind it. The personal attributes are therefore nakedly in front of the community. This situation is further supported by the unavailability of property or paraphernalia, because of the material poverty characteristic of these societies and the need to remain unencumbered in the daily round of life, with its insistent migration.

Yet age and sex are themselves differentiating symbols.

Furthermore, man everywhere can find some means of marking off his personnel: by scarification, initiation, or the ownership of rights to certain songs. None of these burden him or his wife as they move about in search of food. The Australian Arunta, for example, symbolize masculine status by a series of initiatory rituals which move a person through at least four major age categories, and only in the last does he obtain the full privileges of citizenship. Thus, for instance, only the men who have attained the last in this series (and this is often relatively late in life) can view the holy churinga (elaborately decorated oval slabs of polished stone or elongated pieces of hardwood, in which dwell the ancestral spirits as well as the spirits of living Arunta) hidden in a sacred cave, and partake of the ultimate mystery of their existence. Man's ingenuity in devising symbolic means of differentiating one person from another is great; he is not stopped by the want of material things.

One value reappears among hunting and food-gathering peoples: generosity. On the Andaman Islands a man is supposed to give away most of his kill to the people in his band, and the pattern of generosity extends to all the things he owns. Even his child may be handed over to another couple which has expressed a wish for him. Among the Eskimos, food and possessions are freely borrowed and loaned, and the pattern of generosity extends even to a man's wives. Among the Arunta, the sharing of food is more clearly directed toward specified relatives, for here the genius of the society manifests itself in orienting all interactions on the basis of real or imputed kinship. Yet these Australians, no easygoing people, must also share food. There can be little doubt that these demands for generosity in food are functionally necessary. Without storage facilities and with constant movement, game would spoil while people were going hungry if each hearth group cared only for its own. Starvation in the midst of plenty is a luxury that small societies cannot afford, so that some institution of sharing of large game animals is necessary.

When a people have a more settled and plentiful mode of life, prestige symbols become more prominent and are often heavily elaborated, not only because they are available, but because they are useful. People associated in daily intercourse under these conditions are not so intimately known to one another. Personal attributes are not known to the public and may be masked by inherited or acquired symbols of status.

Certain prestige elements tend to recur. One focus of attention is upon agricultural productive capacity, often viewed as magical or spiritual rather than as a matter of skill. A productive farmer is apt to gain status and demonstrate his gains with feasting and other forms of conspicuous display, of which the rotting piles of yams among certain Melanesian tribes offer the best example.

As farming is often in the hands of women and hunting becomes a secondary but still important occupation, we find that military prowess comes to play a large role in the value orientation of men. It is at this horticultural level that the hunting of heads and the taking of scalps most frequently appear as symbols of personal accomplishment.

Land, on the other hand, is often less significant to individual status. Though we will have to examine some special cases, in most instances among horticulturists land is not individually owned, nor does land serve as a social marker. Despite Malinowski's elaborate discussion of the varied rights to land, it is clear that the size of the plot a person holds or uses is not a factor in his prestige; he is more concerned with his productive capacity. Among the Bemba and Ba-Ila of Northern Rhodesia, land is all nominally possessed by the chief, though clearly the occupant has an unassailable use right. But it is a use right, and not a symbol of social worth.

Slash-and-burn cultivation varies under varying conditions with different crops. Thus in plantain growing areas, the groves remain productive for as much as thirty years, and under such circumstances land rights can take on greater meaning. Joel Hester reports that in the southern Maya region the land need lie fallow only for three or four years and apparently by aboriginal methods could be cultivated for five or six successive years. Yet elsewhere, the land is completely abandoned after a single usage, so that no sense of continuity is found, and this seems to be the more characteristic pattern of operation at the horticultural level. In some areas, the land available around a village is used up after twenty or thirty years, and the whole village must move to a new area where fresh bush may be cut. Certain Borneo peoples have elaborate houses made of hand-hewn planks, and these are periodically dismantled and floated downstream to some location where land is available and where they are again set up. Under these variant conditions land can have more or less permanent value and its role as a motivating element varies accordingly.

Where livestock is held in association with horticulture (notably cattle in those parts of Africa south of the Sahara where the tsetse fly is not prevalent and pigs in Melanesia) the men usually have control of the animals, and livestock ownership is an important prestige marker. Where livestock is the sole or major economic resource, these take on a yet more important role as a value symbol, and all life and all prestige tend to revolve around the ownership of herds. The value patterns of herding peoples seem to be consistent. Not only is there emphasis upon livestock as a major value symbol, but repeatedly there tends to be an emphasis upon warfare, quickness of action, harshness in interpersonal relations, and personal arrogance. There appears to be a kind of natural selection for what might be called masculine hardness rather than for feminism.

Where land takes on permanent usefulness and people are settled and begin crowding in on the land, a shift to new values can be seen. Land takes on a dominant value, and characteristically among peasants it serves as the focus of motivation and action. The hunger for land is great in practically every peasant society, and land ownership tends to set the position of the individual. Social institutions revolve around landholding. It is in the continuity of land rights that the recurrent peasant emphasis upon family solidarity and generational continuity can best be understood.

While the peasant emphasis upon land is clearly marked, even where there is but a use right rather than ownership, the development of states and cities proliferates a variety of social patterns with other value orientations. In primitive political states, legal rights to land may rest in the hands of urban residents with political power. This was clearly the case in feudal Europe. According to Baganda law, the Kabaka, as the king was called, theoretically owned all the land. In both cases, of course, established rights to its use were in the hands of the peasants. Land rights therefore are not only a peasant value, but an urban one as well.

The values of the urban residents and of the political elite are often highly elaborated—particularly in the more primitive states. There is usually a clearly marked differentiation of status groups—classes or castes—with separate life modes and public symbols, as well as economic circumstances. The upper echelons usually place emphasis upon leisure and leisure-class activities, including a marked degree of conspicuous consumption. Elaborated symbols to demonstrate these divergences of status are found in all the state systems of preindustrial society, whether in Africa, Middle America, the Near East, India, China, Japan, or Europe. Services, from those of porters to concubines, take a prominent part, while clothes, household trappings, personal ornamentation, and, above all, freedom from useful labors are nearly universal elements in the symbol systems expressing the divergent values in urban and state organized populations.

This demand for services and goods on the part of the developing upper social echelons probably first brought about the aggregation of people that formed towns and cities. Here a number of factors go hand in hand. The development of a power group, the desire for goods, the increased specialization of labor, and hence of social function, are all elements in the growth of political power and urban communities. Under such circumstances, the divergent sectors of the population tend to form separate social groups, each with its own value system. Thus a society emerges in which the people have a variety of value orientations at the same time. Yet the clearly established control in the hands of a limited group and the requisites for exchange of goods generally combine to create some common denominators for the value systems. Large bodies of dispossessed laborers with no land or other regular source of material and cultural satisfactions may appear. To such urban classes, usually slaves, the social values are not attainable. Such sectors of the population may live under circumstances where no values, not even limited ones, are attainable. If they are given no psychological support through religious beliefs or similar mechanisms, if they have neither strong internal ties to the class nor external ones to their masters or employers, they become a population without values. It is this condition which the French sociologist Emile Durkheim called *anomie,* a "social disease" characterized by lack of recognized norms for behavior and, we would add, lack of values. Something similar was expressed by the American anthropologist and linguist, Edward Sapir, in his famous essay, "Culture, Gen-

uine and Spurious." But societies with large urban populations can afford to allow people to starve to death, whereas
hunting and food-gathering peoples cannot.

Industrial conditions of the modern world presage an
alteration of these patterns. The clearest emphasis here
is on the decline of manual work through the increased
availability of mechanical aids and through the correlative
tendency toward the professionalization of all occupations.
The movement has only begun, and only in science fiction
do we glimpse a future in which nobody must soil his hands
or demean himself with physical toil. Yet certainly the
proportion of population freed from dirty or vulgar tasks
has increased markedly. Even the semiskilled factory worker
in modern communities spends his life in neat surround-
ings and with only a moderate expenditure of physical effort. At the same time, mass-produced commodities, produced on the assumption of an increasingly broad mass
market, deprive goods of their function as status markers
and thereby lessen their function as value symbols. The
concept of a silk-stocking set is already outmoded by the
general use of nylons; furs promise to follow a similar
route, and only close control maintains the value function
for diamonds. As this is being written, popular magazines
are printing articles about the decline of the car as a symbol of prestige in America; but it is still too early to know
if this is a temporary or a permanent de-emphasis. What
new values will arise is still a matter of speculation. The
most likely guess is that they will rest chiefly on high-level
technical competence, for the requirements of modern industrial life make necessary a large and ever-growing cadre
of specialists to develop and man the increasingly complicated apparatus that makes modern society viable.

THE EVOLUTION OF STATUS

Two biological facts are fixed upon to differentiate individual status in all societies: age and sex. Thus the expectations of life vary between male and female, and change as
one grows from infancy to old age. Each culture has its own
differentials, its own emphases, yet there is some homo-
geneity among them. In all hunting and food-gathering
societies the search for large game is a masculine occupation; gathering fruits, roots, and shellfish is primarily the
province of women. Warfare, too, is a male occupation,
with only the rarest exceptions, and these at the higher
levels of social development. Our contemporary attitude
toward men and women as being culturally interchangeable may in fact represent their intellectual and biological
potentials, but ethnologically there have been certain
broad consistencies in the definition of the role and the
status of men and women. At both primitive and advanced
levels, men tend regularly to dominate women. But
we must recognize that, whatever hostility may occur between the sexes—and it is markedly recurrent—every social
system requires that the sexes collaborate intimately and
that a measure of give and take exist between the two.

Among horticulturalists the farming operations are
largely in the hands of women, with a few notable exceptions. Hunting and warfare are the major occupations of
men. Not infrequently the men engage in elaborate economic pursuits, the ends of which appear to be the prestigeful bargaining for coveted value symbols. For instance
on the island of Alor (an Indonesian island near Java) the
elaborate bargaining operations for bronze gongs and other
paraphernalia which have little function and less intrinsic
value but which appear to exist only as markers in the

game of conflict for prestige, is an example of a pattern of life where the men have been caught up in elaborate prestige-directed activity. Similar developments of elaborate exchange activities are found among some of the cattle-keeping horticulturalists in Africa and in many other quarters of the earth. Almost everywhere that livestock are kept in great numbers, it is the special prerogative of the men to handle them, and stock ownership comes to be an important value symbol. This is particularly true in herding societies, but it is also true among many of the horticulturalists who have cattle or pigs.

Where the economy allows for larger populations and a more densely settled existence, and particularly where states exist, farming tends to come into the hands of the men. This is true in the Old World, where it is associated with livestock, but it is also true in much of the New World. Why this should be the case is not entirely clear, but I am inclined to the opinion that it is a secondary consequence of the loss of other occupations among the men, particularly the elimination of hunting and the reduction of warfare among the peasants themselves, and possibly also the loss of opportunity for independent prestigeful bargaining.

The history of the Cossacks illustrates the point. Previously organized into military units, devoting their life to hunting, fishing, and warfare, they eventually took to a more settled form of life. In the earlier epoch of their history the women engaged in the farming operations, and the society had a matrilineal bias; when they were forced or seduced into more peaceful life, the men took over the farming operations and the society developed a distinctly patrilineal cast.

The idea should not surprise us, inasmuch as we have witnessed over the past few decades something of the reverse process. European and American women, who had a heavy economic involvement in farm production in an agricultural society, were deprived of their economic role first by movement to the cities and second by the increase of domestic aids. It was in this context that the feminist movement took shape, and particularly among urban middle-class women, life became directed toward the pursuit of success. The feminist movement significantly involved the right to engage in important economic activity.

In all societies, such governance as exists tends to be in the hands of the men, even where there is a strong female bias expressed in rules of matrilineal descent and control of the household by the women. Whether this results from man's general average superior physical strength, from freedom from the demands of gestation and child rearing, or from some other sexual characteristics, most decision making involving the total community, as distinct from the household, lies in masculine hands. Perhaps it is no more than an evolutionary development out of warfare—a masculine operation—to which governance is closely allied.

The emoluments of status vary. In the absence of goods among hunting and food-gathering societies, they cannot be very great. The generosity pattern among the Andamanese is coupled with a pattern of deference toward age, so that older persons get the more choice foods and also more than they give. Among the Arunta, the sexual privileges tend to go to the older men, considerably to the dismay of the young men who have a hard time finding wives. But by and large, status must be its own reward. Increasing emoluments, in the form of special privileges, deference, and increased amenities of life are characteristic at the middle ranges in the evolution of society. These do not, as a rule, include the opportunity to enjoy freedom from the basic economic pursuits. Differentials of status, in terms other than age and sex, are virtually absent; but where settled life prevails, some clear distinctions in prestige do usually occur, and it is possible to speak loosely of social classes. These classes are not clearly demarked but represent the kind of distinctions in status that we have in modern America. Rarely is there any true leisure-class group, for all persons engage in the basic economic pursuits; but there may be hereditary titles to leadership, considerable differences in the control of prestige symbols, and even some opportunity to have personal services performed.

It is under early systems of state organization that status distinctions are most elaborate and most clearly demarcated. Rare, indeed, is the nascent political system that does not provide for elaborate delineations of social differentiation and explicit sumptuary regulations to maintain the public expression of these distinctions. With the development of state systems, the manifest rewards of status are emphasized. Special foods, personal services, elaborate protocol, special vessels, clothes, and houses, multiple wives to which are added concubines, all make the rewards of status resplendent. The *reductio ad absurdum* of such a pattern is where, as in some West African states, the king is so surrounded by the demands of deference that he is literally immobilized—a prisoner of his own prestige.

The modern world has inherited the legacy of differentials created under more primitive political conditions, though these have been eroded by the increasing importance of industrial production and shifting foci of power. The diversity of technical competences and the multifaceted pattern of economic and social life have resulted in a variety of special statuses. The older economic system has been undermined by the further proliferation of special activities, each person operating in terms of the general market place, through which his economic satisfactions are met and to which he contributes. As economic relationships take on this market character, it follows that social interactions will also do so, and public status (as distinct from private intrafamilial and other close personal involvements) likewise takes on a market character. Thus status tends to be defined in pecuniary terms: What does the man have? As for most persons this is a result of occupation, it is also expressed in terms of occupational categories, so that, whereas a Tlingit Indian or an Australian Arunta will establish contact with a stranger by determining clan affiliation or putative kinship, a modern American will ask the broad yet specific question: What does the man do? Aside from occupation (which may be symbolized by special forms of dress or by language), public expenditures, such as cars, clothes, houses, and leisure pursuits are often status cues.

THE EVOLUTION OF SOCIAL ROLES

At the more primitive levels, role is generally a matter of kinship, sex, and age. Few official roles exist; and often the relation of each person to every other is primarily one of some real or imputed degree of consanguinity. The only other roles of importance are the role of strangers (i.e. enemies) and the role of the religious practitioners, which will be discussed later. The importance of kinship in determining relations between people continues in an absolute sense for most social systems, though, as we have already seen, role patterns between kin of the same kind vary from one culture to the next. The major decline occurs with the development of urban life and industrialization, and even here, according to recent studies, kinship continues to serve important functions in the relationships among persons. Kinship is nowhere erased from the consciousness of mankind, and the appropriate relationship between kin is established as a recognized social role; the only important difference is that the proportion that kin relationships constitute of all the relationships that each person has is constantly declining.

Under the more settled conditions of hunters and food-gatherers, and particularly among horticulturalists, there is a tendency to develop certain special roles. This is particularly true with respect to leadership functions, and this factor continues to develop as political organization becomes increasingly complex. To some extent the special groups and the emergence of a degree of occupational specialization also create particularistic roles. Where clans exist, as has already been shown, clan membership is often a determinant of role position, as each person takes a degree of personal responsibility for the clan welfare and must orient his life around his clan's needs. Under such conditions we occasionally see the emergence of role conflict between the demands of the clan and more personal interests. There is evidence of such tension in the patterns of inheritance under the matrilineal clan system of the Tlingit, where a man's status cannot be passed to his own son, and also where clan loyalty contravenes the potential mutual interest between husband and wife. On the other hand, important role distinctions within a clan may be found, for so large a unit must have leadership to maintain its integrity and to guide the course of common clan action. Again with the Tlingit, we find what to us is the anomalous situation in which one house may contain at once the very highest and very nearly lowest statuses, and these not as servant and master but as nephew and uncle, broadly speaking.

Official roles proliferate with the development of political organization, while occupational roles also become increasingly important. These continue to grow under industrial patterns of organization, so that in the modern world they tend to overwhelm social interaction. With higher concentration of population, each person comes into contact with an increasingly large number of others, but does so in a more particular way. Thus the individual sees his fellows increasingly in some particular light, as boss or merchant, as servant or ruler, and not in terms of his total social existence. In turn he shows only one face to his public. Only in the confines of his immediate social environs, e.g., the family or some particularly close group of associates, does a person have generic involvement. And under this condition symbol systems take on an increasing importance. In industrial society this pattern is furthered in that even a man's primary role in the economy may be obscure, as when he works on an assembly line and becomes little more than a statistic to all but a few chance associates. Under these conditions the market place, in which so much interaction occurs, becomes completely depersonalized into the supermarket, and the connection between persons is increasingly defined in pecuniary terms. This depersonalization of interaction leaves unsatisfied the desire for positive affect, so that the individual is constrained to seek other sources of intimacy and to find a means for public display of individuality as well as of status. It is these losses of established social role and the compensatory actions that people take which have largely been responsible for both sociological and literary discussions of the evils of urban life, of, in Freud's classic phrase, the problem of "civilization and its discontents."

THE EVOLUTION OF AUTHORITY SYSTEMS

It follows from what has already been said that authority patterns among hunting and food-gathering peoples are weak and limited in scope. Such power for decision as exists —and it is never entirely wanting—generally rests in the hands of senior men, usually as a group, though there may be a single head. It never reaches beyond the band or village, except when a charismatic leader, endowed with those virtues that his society particularly values, may emerge from time to time. A. R. Radcliffe-Brown informs us that a young Andaman Islander who is a good hunter, who is active, and who properly displays the Andamanese virtues of generosity and deference could become a kind of leader of men from several different bands, despite his youth. Similar patterns were found among California Indians.

There is never juridical authority under these conditions. That is, the parties to disputes that arise between individuals within a band, or between two bands, have no person or group to which they regularly turn for a resolution of their conflict. To be sure, means are available by which the parties to such conflict can bargain for a peaceable settlement and the community can give its sanction to the decision—and may even enforce its fulfillment—once the parties have come to an agreement. But this is different from a rendered judgment. There is no recognized power, either in the community at large or in the hands of an individual, to claim jurisdiction or to render a judgment. For example, the famous song and wrestling duels of the Eskimos are a nonviolent means of resolving conflict, and those present may give encouragement and make acceptance of the outcome a matter of pressure; but the community has no office. Again, the old men among the Arunta of Australia, may, as Spencer and Gillen describe, work things out so that the individuals who have done something contrary to expected behavior are punished, but they have no actual authority to do so. Under these conditions, authority is resolved by direct conflict or by ritualized or formalized conflict (duel) through which the two parties come to terms. The community and the elite may express themselves in support of a decision; they do not enforce it. The elite may have a means of withholding rewards thereby demanding conformity. The Arunta elders who have gone through the full initiation cycle may indefinitely withhold the final initiation from a man who does not behave properly. But this type of control is over general behavior, not over specific disputes.

With advancement in cultural development, one or both of two instruments of broader power may emerge: the clan and the secret societies of men. Secret societies, with their privilege of membership and often with tight internal control and marked grades differentiating status, may have a profound influence on the behavior of non-initiates and initiates alike. They may form a means of unity extending over a wide area as well. The clan institutions are more frequent. These wield power internally through paternalistic or avuncular control and through strong sentiments of unity that hold the members together. As clans usually extend over several local units, they serve also to weld these smaller geographical entities into a kind of unity. On the other hand, a characteristic of clans is that each tends to be a sovereign entity, bound to peaceful co-existence and mutual interdependence (furthered by the necessity of intermarriage) but not recognizing any superior authority with decision-making powers over the separate clans. Yet the dual ties—one to the local area in which the person lives, the other to the kin group spread out into surrounding areas—frequently make for cohesion and the beginning of some kind of political sense, though not for true political institutions.

For instance, juridical matters involving separate clans tend always to be clan affairs, and thus individual disputes are involved with these larger political alignments. Even though the leaders do not place decision making in the hands of some person or groups, they regularly bargain out the minor disturbances and reach peaceable agreements through statesmanship. Sometimes their actions take place in regular councils of clan leaders. This pattern reached its most highly elaborated condition among the Iroquois. The League maintained a peace for about two centuries, without foregoing sovereignty on the part either of the clan or the tribe, as far as we can tell. (The United Nations concept of the veto, expressed in the League as the vote of unanimity, was the effective instrument. The Iroquois League had the advantage over the UN, however, of being a military alliance that was profitable because it enabled them to exploit surrounding tribes.)

With the advancement of societies into political systems, there is by definition a centralized system of authority. Some scholars believe the origin of such control rested on the development of irrigation agriculture and the need to coordinate the use of water; but it is more likely that state systems came about through a variety of factors in different places. They are not inevitable wherever concentrations of population occur, but they have occurred on every continent except Australia. It seems that both the personal and social motivations for the concentration of power are great and that large political systems will recur under relatively rich and stable agricultural systems but that the institutional problems in maintaining a concentration of power are also great, so that it is difficult to preserve stable state systems.

Among the requisites for maintaining a viable political system are: the development of a public commitment to the centers of power, the creation of channels of authority, the muting of dissident groups and the co-option of that potential dissidence to the purposes of the centers of power, and the regular transmission of power. Nascent states are notably volatile; there is no political history without changing dynasties, shifts in alignments, court intrigue, factionalism, and realignment. Perhaps the growth of industrial economic organization and the more or less popular participation

in government combine to render the advantages of centralized authority sufficiently clear so that the personnel of
modern states increasingly recognize that the continuance
of political institutions is to its own advantage. Loyalties
to political entities can and have been built without any
visible advantage to the rank and file, but certainly they
must not be so easy to preserve as they are where popular
benefit derives from political stability.

Centralized authority requires the provision of an adjudicative system. A political system cannot allow disputes
to be decided among its citizenry by force. That is, if a state
is to exist, it must have monopoly on the legitimate use
of force and the means to protect itself against its private
use. This is one reason why the organization of states is inimical to the continuance of clans, for in a full clan system,
authority and the balance of action rest on recourse to
armed combat by separate sovereign clans. A state takes
over this function.

The Baganda illustrate this point very nicely where,
before European intervention a century ago, quite apparently a struggle was taking place between the older clans
and the centralized political system, in which the clans had
been the losers. This is the most reasonable interpretation
of two factors in Baganda social life. One was the specific
regulation that all disputes must be channeled through
the hierarchy of courts provided by the government. The
other was the official concept that land was actually owned
by the Kabaka, while at the same time the clans endeavored
to maintain and extend their clan lands through certain
more-or-less ritual means. The Kabaka had the better of it,
but apparently the price he paid was eternal vigilance.

Central authority also leads to bureaucratization. That
is, unification of large areas means that there must be a
channel of command, that officials must be appointed and
authority delegated. Older institutions may be employed,

as among the West African Ashanti where the older lineage system provided the hierarchy of chiefs leading from the local village up to the *Asantahene,* the paramount chief. The building up of larger political entities through alignments of local leaders, each controlling his own population through established ties, appears to be the central element in feudal types of organization. Institutions may also be created more or less *de novo,* as apparently was the Baganda pattern, where the intermediate levels of rulers served at the pleasure of the Kabaka by whom they were appointed.

The problem of authority is to some extent alleviated by the tendency of the rank and file of a population to continue its own life within the confines of the peasant community, paying its taxes and tithes (and grumbling) as hostage to the powers that be, in order that it may be left alone with its own domestic concerns. If the central authority does not make too great demands in the form of taxes, draft, corvée, or sheer banditry, the bargain has its advantages in the form of relative peace and quiet. If the technology is sufficiently advanced, so that true economic advantages are obtained through the division of labor, the result can be advantageous to everyone, though there is a clear and recurrent tendency for the peasant to be exploited by the centers of power, whether these be political or commercial.

Industrialization has brought about broader political participation. This appears to be a product of society's growing requirement for a large body of skilled persons and an increased variety and specification of skills, particularly the creative ones. Such personnel must be drawn widely from the population, rather than from an elite group. Moreover, the crucial role that particular occupational groups can bring to bear—as distinct from an undifferentiated peasantry or a mass of foot soldiers—places new vulnerabilities on the central power. Where the ancient world had to make compromises between religious and secular leadership, where the Aztecs had to draw the merchants into their elite, where the industrialists of the eighteenth and nineteenth centuries were necessarily given increased power in European states, it is now necessary to recognize the potentials of a wide variety of specific laboring groups, because of the thoroughgoing interdependence of all aspects of life. Each group, like the women in the *Lysistrata* of Aristophanes (a case which is duplicated among the women of the Ba-Ila of northern Rhodesia), potentially can threaten the continuity of the social system. The centers of power cannot allow for the alienation of any major group; it must either force conformity to its de mands or bargain for it.

IDEOLOGICAL DEVELOPMENT

The religion of hunting and food-gathering peoples is dominated by shamanism and the belief in a world of spirits. The only religious practitioner found in most of these groups is the shaman, as anthropologists (borrowing a Siberian Tungus word) call the persons who influence the spirits for good and evil. The shaman is a man (occasionally also a woman and in some societies only women) who has acquired, by special indoctrination or initiation, the power to control the spirits which bring sickness and death. He cures illness among his friends and causes it among his enemies. He is therefore generally feared and respected for his power and often has a potent influence on community affairs. His is often a special status with a special role in these societies; he may be powerful and, if the society has surplus goods, quite wealthy. But he also engages in the normal economic routine of his tribe. Why this form of religious activity is so widespread among hunters and food-gatherers and is submerged at higher levels is something of an enigma. Some kind of control over the spirit world is found in all societies, however, even in our own highly pragmatic one.

Aside from shamanism all such peoples have elaborated beliefs with regard to the nature of the world, its origin, and the place of man within it. These beliefs involve the recognition of a personal soul or spirit, as well as external (frequently malevolent) ones; beyond this, little generalization is possible. What we can say is merely that the world of the unknown must everywhere be faced, and that its mysterious workings are made explicable by the provision of beings or substances with the capacity to act, and that through the shaman some of these supernatural events can be predicted and controlled.

Social distinctions at this level which, as already noted, rest chiefly on age and sex, are regularly marked by rituals. Puberty rites for girls are probably universal, while puberty ceremonies for boys are frequent. These latter may be highly elaborated, as among the Arunta, where the series of ceremonies begins before puberty and ends well after a man is mature. Such rituals mark off the important distinctions between sexes, often symbolize the secrecy of men's affairs, and occasionally express outright hostility toward women. They also mark off differentials of age.

Other rituals mark birth, marriage, parenthood, and death. These *rites of passage* (as A. van Gennep called them) from one status to the next not only convey to the public that the individual has attained a new status, but they also increase his own awareness of that changed status and its concomitant role. Frequently the ritual itself, or some explicit verbalizations in it, communicates new obligations and privileges to the initiate. The importance of such rituals for a people who have no other means of recording events can be very great, for they serve notice to all in a manner that is not easily forgotten by any. Rituals involving the whole community, called *rites of intensification,* re-enforce the initiate's sense of belonging and serve to strengthen group ties. Such rituals always have religious overtones and can be found in all social systems at all levels, but are most important at the more primitive level.

Horticultural communities may have animistic beliefs but usually also have more developed cult activities and often a priest, i.e., a person whose special task it is to conduct group rituals. Where clans prevail, there is generally some belief in special clan spirits. In various parts of the world these beliefs have taken the form of totemism, wherein the clan is viewed as spiritually associated or actually one with some species of animal, plant, or some natural phenomenon like rain or lightning. This association involves a sacred identity (often expressed as a tabu against eating the animal which gives the group its name), but from the sociological point of view serves as a sort of emblem of group unity. Special clan ancestors are usually propitiated and special clan rituals give unity to the group. Other cults may also be found; often the secret societies have a religious basis or rationale involving special ritual activities. In short, both religious belief and religious practices relate to the established patterns of social organization.

The development of the state usually involves the spiritual prerogative of rule on the part of the centers of power (though inevitably this sanction is supported by more tangible use of force). Under these circumstances, priestcraft is apt to become extremely important, and few if any states have existed prior to our own which did not have an elaborated religion intimately tied to the sources of secular power, from which it got ideological sustenance and to which it gave support.

Religious ideology in state systems, in sanctioning the right to power of the elite, also tends to justify existing conditions for others, particularly the peasant population. It carries to them a note of fatalism, a note that the conditions of life are a part of the natural order of things. Such state-oriented religion is frequently of secondary importance to the peasants themselves, for their interests and therefore their religions are concerned with the fertility of their land, beasts, and women. Their magical practices put them close to the primitive world, from which we may presume most of the attitudes and practices derive. The fatalistic character of Catholic doctrine, together with its ready syncretism of pre-existing religious beliefs, has appealed to peasant populations over a good part of the world for many centuries. Catholicism as an ideology and a social institution seems particularly well adapted to peasant community life.

On the other hand, modern capitalism does not find a fatalistic point of view congenial. The emphasis upon man's mastery of his environment and the express demand that each individual determine his own fate was rationalized in capitalism by its principal spokesman, Adam Smith, in the idea that society is best served when each person seeks his own self-interest. Such an economic philosophy demands an appropriate religious ideology. This was supplied by Protestantism. The functional relationship between the urban commercial economic order and the Protestant ethic, as expressed by Tawney and Weber, has already been noted.

This ideology, in turn, has been a major force in support of the scientific spirit that dominates the Western world today, a new ideology that grew out of the concepts of human mastery and independence. And modern science has carried the industrial revolution forward, so that our whole social structure is undergoing further major changes. We do not know what ideologies will emerge to support the future world, where societies become increasingly massive and social action more bureaucratized and where scientific understanding and man's mastery of the physical world will be more complete. Nazi Germany and communist Russia have tried to develop popular ideologies which justify established systems of power and give a religious mystique to the state as an entity. Tendencies to nationalistic ideologies appear in all modern nations, and they may be effective means of developing mass loyalties, whether or not they suit our personal tastes. But an ideology must do more than justify an existing order; it must provide proper motivations for the people as a whole. In the modern world this means, among other things, making its personnel willing to undertake those tasks which are necessary for the functioning of the society as a whole.

The growth of technology involves change in the life circumstances of the population. It tends to create changes in the concentration of population, the accumulation of goods, the degree to which people may lead a settled life, their opportunities for leisure, and an increase in the area over which there is communication. These changed circumstances in turn require and make possible divergent ways of meeting the imperatives of all social systems. Though no society is a perfectly functioning mechanism, the institutions of society are instrumentalities through which group life can be maintained and through which the individual can be supplied with minimally necessary satisfactions of both his physical needs and his culturally conditioned wants.

Whatever the nature of the society, the social imperatives continue. But the pattern in which they operate will vary, and this variation is dependent, in large measure, on the character of that technology and the size and circumstances of the population that it supports. For this reason, the institutions of society undergo evolutionary change.

The Evolution of Society

ON EVOLUTIONARY STAGES

CLASSIC evolutionary theory involves a listing of the evolutionary stages in human development. Can a modern evolutionary formulation be expressed in stages, too? Evolution is a developmental concept, and development consists in gradual modification rather than in the abrupt leaps which a set of stages implies. Yet the nature of language and thought imposes upon us a taxonomy of presumed discrete entities through which the process is viewed: the mind must infer movement from a series of stills, as the eye does with motion pictures. This is not to say that there is no validity in the stages themselves but rather that they must not be treated with the rigidity of truly discrete entities.

Evolution is a gradual process largely because the evolution of technology is made up of an infinite series of inventions and improvements, each giving to its possessors some minor advantage but, with rare exceptions, not completely altering the life mode of the people. The development of the automobile, a technological device with important and well-advertised social concomitants, illustrates that even in our day of explosive change innovation has been gradual. The development of agriculture better demonstrates that such influences are not merely a single step in the improvement of man's food-producing capacity, but that they emerge through innumerable minor discoveries and inventions: a process that is still taking place.

The second reason why a series of discrete stages cannot be rigidly established is that technology is only one factor in an equation that involves environment as well. The productive capacity of land, to return to the agricultural example, is certainly a matter associated with technical competence; but it is also a matter of the quality of the soil, the precipitation, the growing season, and a host of other factors which man has until now been able to change only in a most limited way. Under certain circumstances, in fact, the productive potential of resources already existing in nature may be greater in some areas than the productive potential of primitive farming is in another. If we consider that the development of technology is the prime mover in social evolution and that it operates on the social level through changing population density, settlement patterns, economic well-being, and the like, then it follows that this evolution is not simply a matter of stages of set character. Rather, there are infinite degrees of development, and these in turn are subjected to factors external to the sociocultural system which here and there alter the underlying regularity.

Yet, a taxonomy of societies based upon the manner in which a people exploit their environment to obtain their basic needs is not entirely off the mark, for, broadly speaking and with these reservations in mind, these productive techniques fulfill the basic needs of human sustenance and set the conditions to which a host of secondary circumstances must conform. For example, not only does agriculture ordinarily provide a type of resource and a general level of food supply, but it does so in a particular way with particular demands, such as requirements of work, localization in space, the importance of land, the preservation of seed, and similar factors.

In short, evolutionary stages must be seen as a first approximation to a taxonomy of cultures based upon the development of economic resources.

THE ECONOMIC BASIS OF AN EVOLUTIONARY TAXONOMY

The old three-stage theory of classic evolution distinguishes between the "savagery" of hunting and food-gathering societies, the "barbarism" of simple hoe and digging-stick horticulturists, and the "civilization" resting on the use of more advanced farming techniques. Without subscribing to the values implicit in this old-fashioned terminology, a modern classification can be built upon this system. But the classification may be rendered more accurate by subdivisions related to evolutionary stages:

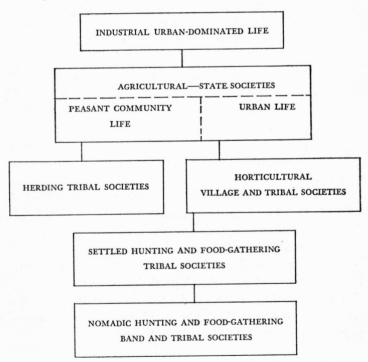

These categories are presented in their evolutionary sequence, that is, with the most primitive at the bottom and
the most advanced at the top, following the tradition of
geology and archeology. We will treat each category in
detail in the remainder of the chapter; here it is necessary
only to point up some general characteristics of the schema.

The first two categories represent pretty much what were
once called savagery; i.e., peoples who exploit the natural
environment, but do not produce their food. They fall into
two broad categories: those whose technology is so poor or
whose environment is so deficient that they must move
about in search of food and therefore live in camps, and
those more advanced (or more fortunate) who can have
permanent villages and larger populations.

The middle categories are what were once called barbarians. They are made up of two quite different types.
One is the horticulturists, who live by gardening, have no
advanced techniques of food production and generally remain on a tribal level of social organization. This is presumably an earlier economic mode than true agriculture.
The second is the herding societies, i.e., peoples keeping
herds or flocks in arid regions, and whose life is dominated
by the needs of their animals, off which they live. It repre-
sents a special ecologic adjustment, involving life modes
and social organization comparable to the horticultural
level. Archeological evidence suggests that the domestication and handling of grazing animals was accomplished
by fully developed agriculturists, and that nomadic herding does not therefore derive either directly from a hunting
stage nor out of horticulture. Therefore we view nomadic
herding as a kind of devolution to something more primitive, as a result of ecologic adaptation.

The remaining two categories bring us to what the older
writers called civilization. The development of agriculture
makes for internal division, as indicated. The older agri-

cultural societies are giving way to industrial societies, dominated economically by the urban products.

These stages are a typology of basic ecological forms and represent the major classes of social systems as they appear in an evolutionary sequence. Within such stages, social life will tend to be alike in its basic structure and character, though made of different cultural details. For their similarity derives from similarity of circumstance and functional fitness, not from common cultural heritage. The social imperatives will tend to find similar solutions.

NOMADIC HUNTING AND FOOD-GATHERING SOCIETIES

There is no reason to suppose that the earliest man had anything but a nomadic hunting and food-gathering system. In every major land area a few of these still exist, and there is no reason to believe that these nomadic gatherers ever had any other form of life. There are a few possible exceptions, such as the Siriono of eastern Bolivia, where internal evidence suggests that a secondary readaptation to pure hunting and food-gathering was made by a formerly horticultural people. These hunting and food-gathering societies therefore stand at the bottom of our evolutionary schema. This is not, however, to say that the contemporary examples illustrate the primordial character of man—most certainly not—or that their cultures have been unchanged in the millennia of their existence. It suggests rather that the common and recurrent elements in their social system offer us the closest approximation to the earliest form of human social life that can be reconstructed on the basis of ethnographic data.

Nomadic hunting and food-gathering societies are still found in widely scattered parts of the globe. (Unless otherwise noted, when discussing the distribution of cultures in modern times, we refer to the time of first European contact—which varies in different parts of the world. Many of these aboriginal people have taken over European ways during the past century, and some, like the Tasmanians, have become extinct.) They are characteristic of all Australian aborigines and the little island of Tasmania, which is the true land's end of the world for it is most remote from the centers of high culture, where the most primitive recorded human technology is found. Some Australians in very favorable locations appear to have become settled hunters, but we know little of their culture.

Nomadic hunting and food-gathering societies are also found in the southern tip of the South American continent, notably in Tierra del Fuego, and occasionally in the jungles of the Amazon (though again, our data are very meager and uncertain, due to the long influence of Europeans and the sparse and conflicting accounts left to us). In North America, hunting and food-gathering was found throughout Alaska, except the panhandle, and Canada, except for the southeastern sector and the west coast, on the plains before adoption of the horse, in the intermountain region of the West, and into the northern arid portion of Mexico. The Far West, from southeastern Alaska to central California, was occupied by peoples who lived a settled hunting and food-gathering life.

In Africa, nomadic hunting and food-gathering peoples are now found only on the Kalahari Desert (the Bushmen) and in the jungles of the Congo basin (the Pygmies). There are scattered peoples throughout southern Asia, all pygmies or pygmoid, who appear to have had no agriculture whatsoever, though some of them have long had close contact with farming peoples and have adopted horticultural practices from them. In Siberia there are also peoples who do no farming. There is considerable evidence that in all these sectors of the world, except Australia and possibly the

Amazon basin, the area of hunting and food-gathering has been consistently declining during the centuries prior to the European dispersal of population, which has further reduced them drastically.

The general characteristics of nomadic hunting and food-gathering societies are these: they are formed into bands of from twenty to fifty persons who camp together, share a territory which they protect from enemy invasion, and interact with other coequal bands inhabiting contiguous but separate territories. Each band is part of a larger social group which we may call a tribe, but this tribe has no organization or unity beyond a vague sense of belonging expressed by its constituent members. The band is subdivided into families or hearth groups, a marital couple (extra wives usually are permitted, but only had by a limited portion of the men), and their immature and unmarried children. The individual family (or sometimes groups of closely related families) may split off into separate units under dire economic circumstances, but the band usually remains together throughout the year. In extremely impoverished geographical areas, such as part of the Eskimo country and the American Southwestern desert, the sense of territorial unity may be wanting and the band may not be a continuous functioning entity. Nevertheless, most characteristically the band is the core of social unity and action.

As we have already seen, status and role relations in hunting and food-gathering societies rest upon age, sex, and kin; men tend to dominate women, the old to dominate the young. Status differentiation carries only minimal prerogatives; status symbols are unelaborated. Age and sex differentiations are both frequently given ceremonial expression in special initiatory rites which clearly express the individual status and advancement in the essentially age-based social hierarchy.

Values remain personal and direct. Where a population

is close to subsistence, as is usually the case, the knowledge necessary for finding food, skill in hunting, and the requisite energy and industry to do so are likely to loom large. Furthermore, where personal contacts are intimate and continuous, it is not easy to camouflage values behind secondary symbols. Hence, the value system remains close to the valued personal attributes and these in turn remain close to the economically useful abilities. Multiple wives and superior food may serve as status symbols as well as for the satisfaction of appetites, but compared to other systems, the patterns of social distinction remain relatively simple.

Authority rests largely on an informal conclave of senior men; it is limited in extent and lacking in established and recognized coercive power. The old men can carry the support of tradition and bring their superior knowledge into play, or (as among the Arunta) they are the respository of elaborate esoteric knowledge. Such authority as does exist applies only to intraband matters, and among the extremely sparse peoples it is virtually limited to the individual household. It tends to rest upon a traditional right to be heard, upon the control of practical and esoteric knowledge, and perhaps even more on personality. There is no technique for policing such authority, though subterfuges are occasionally to be seen, as, for instance, when the Arunta elders arrange with the enemy to kill only those individuals who have not been living according to the culturally accepted standards. Adjudicative procedure is absent or ill-defined. Some kind of dueling within the band is a recurrent mode of adjudicating disputes, and such recourse to arms is characteristic in any dispute involving more than one band. In some instances this may be formalized and ritualized to give particular sanction to the decision and to reduce actual bloodshed. There is no person with recognized power to enforce settlement, but public opinion may be effective, and frequently (but not always) there are patterned methods of reestablishing amity through formal procedures of redress. Examples of this are the song duel of the Eskimos, a public effort to shame the opponent by means of ad lib derisive songs which, in a sense, state the case and shame the culprit. Ritualized duels among the Australians generally allow for a degree of damage in keeping with the character of the wrong done. Occasionally some superior association (as among some Fuegian tribes) may give a measure of unity to and authority over an area larger than a band, but such unity is weak at best.

Sanctions and beliefs supporting the social order seem to be less clearly defined. The one universal religious feature is the shaman, the practitioner of magical arts controlling health and sickness. He is a focus of power as a result of his special knowledge and his potential use of magic as a threat against wrongs, both within and beyond the band. The support of age and sex differentials is often, as already indicated, elaborated through a series of ceremonials which give validity to this set of differentiations. Rules of social interaction are generally sanctioned by elaborate systems of proper kin relationships which lay down the blueprint for appropriate behavior in most normal, friendly social intercourse.

These are the broad similarities; each people has a separate culture, developed in the course of its own individual history and adapted to its own environment.

SEDENTARY HUNTING AND FOOD-GATHERING SOCIETIES

Truly settled hunters and food-gatherers are now limited to the West Coast of North America, extending from California northward to include southeastern Alaska. They include such California tribes as the Yokuts, Pomo, Patwin, Wintun, and Yuki in central California, the Hupa and

Yurok of northwestern California, the Salish peoples of
Oregon, the Kwakiutl of British Columbia, and the Haida
and Tlingit of southeastern Alaska. Some degree of sedentariness may be found among the Andaman Islanders and
also in parts of Australia; and some South American
peoples, like the Bororo, also seem not to have had agriculture, yet live a sedentary life. But information from
these areas lacks specificity and makes broad comparison
difficult. V. Gordon Childe is at some pains to show that
some paleolithic and mesolithic cultures enjoyed similar
conditions, and suggests that these ancient circumstances
were instrumental in the development of food production.
However that might be, the settled hunters and food-
gatherers often do partake of social patterns similar to
those of peoples who have simple forms of agriculture.
Settled hunters and food-gatherers live in areas where the
natural supply of food is abundant. In California, the chief
source of food was the acorn, an excellent and fairly re-
liable source of nourishment. Northward, berries and roots
and particularly salmon and other resources of the sea and
streams are plentiful enough to supply the basis for large
aggregates of people.

Under these circumstances permanent villages are possible and regularly exist. For the most part, they remain independent, though on the Northwest Coast some unity is
achieved through clans and secret societies which serve to
tie together the separate segments and to give a measure of
cohesion to a broader territory. Thus, the band has been
transformed into a village. This village often has the essential characteristics of the band: a small independent social
entity, its members living close together in a delimited
area and divided into separate families or households
which form its constituent parts. The village differs from
the band in two respects: it occupies a location permanently
through the year and through the generations, and it is

generally somewhat larger, running to the order of a hundred persons.

Occasionally these societies, as well as the horticultural ones, have clans. These large familistic entities, which use sentiments of kinship to bind together wider areas, have already been discussed in some detail. A fully functioning clan forms a kind of corporate group sharing territorial lands; it makes demands on the loyalty of its constituent members, each member being responsible to and for the whole. It may also be specially useful as a landholding entity, serving a broad basis for recognizing and protecting land rights. The clan in fact has some of the legal attributes of a modern corporaton.

Secret societies, which establish class distinction between men and unite members together irrespective of local group, may also give a measure of political unity to otherwise disparate entities. These, too, are infrequent among hunting and food-gathering societies, though the Kuksu cult in central California and the Hamatsa "cannibal" society of the Kwakiutl of British Columbia serve such purposes in a limited way. Clans and secret societies are institutions that integrate and unite people over a wide area; they are characteristic of horticultural peoples, but are also found among settled hunting and food-gathering societies.

Settled life makes possible the accumulation of goods, and throughout the Pacific region such property enters into the system of social distinctions. The form of the wealth and the methods of accumulation and transmission vary, but distinctions of wealth are regular features in the social system of the settled hunters and food-gatherers of this region. Permanent villages and increased leisure make such accumulation possible. Status frequently becomes hereditary and carries with it privileges and prerogatives, including a measure of authority. The peoples in this area,

especially where environmental factors foster larger aggregates and higher levels of living, regularly recognize a
social hierarchy based upon the symbols of prestige in the
form of material goods. Capital, in the sense of material
items that have food-producing usefulness, remains relatively unimportant but is not entirely absent. Land has
more explicit value than among the nomadic hunting and
food-gathering peoples, but not in a form which generally
permits exploitation by individuals or families. (Unique
among hunters and food-gatherers is the elaborate system
of privately held property of the Yurok and their neighbors,
where each person or individual family owns special hunting, fishing, and gathering locations. This situation is made
possible by the unusual character of the economic resources
of this sector of northern California.) Land is generally held
in common, either by the village or some larger familistic
group, such as the clans among the Tlingit. Capital, in the
form of equipment, may occasionally be found; for example
the large, seagoing boats of the Northwest Coast tribes, and
large deer and rabbit nets and fish weirs of the California
Indians, all require considerable investment of labor and
form primary capital equipment. In societies where wealth
is elaborated and is used in the system of social relationships, some form of money or standard measure of value
serves as a medium of exchange.

Although a loose sense of tribal affiliation is found comparable to that of nomadic hunting and food-gathering
societies, and although some measure of integration of
separate units is often provided through clans and secret
societies, there is little or no true political unity, and there
appears to be no case in which large areas are brought under
a single administrative or juridical system with offices vested
with secular powers extending beyond village or clan. Individual charismatic leaders emerge in California tribes, but
institutional support for their continued authority is want-

ing. Juridical action rests on the threat of feud between either individuals, local groups, or clans. Chiefs among the Yokuts of central California had the right to give or withhold permission to a person to exact blood revenge, but even such extremely limited authority is unusual. The distinction between feud and warfare is often difficult to make, for as entities become larger, conflict tends to become warlike In either case, there is likely to be some culturally established means of arriving at an amicable settlement, either before actual fighting starts or when the contestants are ready to quit. Settlement is usually in terms of compensation to the winner, often some form of prestigeful property. Such settlements are sanctioned in custom (or in religion), and have a public aspect to give social meaning to the arrangement. An intermediary may help the parties reach agreement, but there is nobody who can render decision.

HORTICULTURAL SOCIETIES

Peoples who gain their chief livelihood by planting seeds, roots, or tubers and harvesting the product, but who do so without the knowledge of fertilizer, terracing, irrigation, regular rotation of crops, or the use of draft animals, constitute the horticultural societies. Many tribes grow only a portion of their vegetable food (e.g., the Yuman peoples of California and many tribes in the Gran Chaco), and are economically close to the gathering peoples. For practical purposes the primary distinction between horticultural and agricultural economic systems lies in the degree to which their lands are permanently and continuously productive; for the horticulturists open new fields each year, use them for two to four years, and abandon them to bush. The provision of fertilizer is thus not a conscious act but rather a secondary response to the techniques of clearing. This procedure makes possible the development of more or less permanent villages, but it limits both their size and productivity. In this form of production, land does not have permanent value as such but only to the extent that an investment of labor has been made. More accurately, the cost of reclaiming land for horticultural purposes must be amortized over three years rather than projected indefinitely into the future.

Our horticultural category is the broadest and internally the most varied of the lot, and closer examination may ultimately provide sensible and useful subdivisions. In its present form, it appears throughout Oceania (except Australia), is found in limited extent on the Asiatic continent and is characteristic of Africa south of the Sahara. It is found in the eastern United States and northern Mexico and in tropical South America and throughout the intervening regions of Middle America wherever more advanced systems did not prevail. The Pueblos of our Southwest are a special adaptation to extremely arid conditions. Variations in plants used, climate, soils, and extraneous conditions confer variety upon this whole category. Where particularly favorable circumstances exist, a horticultural economy may have the richness and stability that enables it to take on the features generally limited to advanced farming so that (as among the hunters and food-gatherers) special circumstances permit sociological advancement without the concomitant technical proficiency.

Leaving aside these special cases, horticultural societies tend to be organized around village units comparable to those of the more advanced hunting and food-gathering peoples, more frequently bound together with clans and/or secret societies, but without true political unity. Village populations tend to number in the hundreds. In each village there are found a number of clans. Family organization is highly variable but centers around a man and his wives. The division of labor remains simple, but in the majority of cases women do the basic agricultural work, men clear the bush, hunt, fight, and where there are domestic animals, take care of the livestock.

Value orientations tend to focus either on individual productive capacity as among the Trobrianders, or on military prowess, or both. Where livestock is an adjunct, as in much of eastern and southern Africa (cattle) or in Melanesia (pigs), these animals form a prominent part in symbolizing status. Frequently, such animals are used as exchange in the acquisition of wives, multiple wives being a sign of prosperity and a mark of status as well as a source of well-being. Other and varied prestige symbols abound.

In most instances, political structure remains weak and social ties beyond the village and clan do not permit true concerted action. Where they exist, chiefs and councils are limited both in amount of authority and extent of area. Important decisions are generally taken within the clan or some similar delimited social entity and have a paternalistic character. Decisions of broader reach are often in the hands of tribal elders or clan representatives (frequently one and the same). Their decisions are often not fully binding, but again provide a kind of trucelike arrangement, wherein each clan or other segment may resort to the lance when not satisfied with the course of events. As we will see in the subsequent section, state organized societies have developed among horticultural peoples, but it is not clear whether the concept of state organization can arise under these conditions, though the evidence from the New World suggests that it can.

Where environmental conditions are favorable for productive hoe cultivation and relatively permanent land use, and where they are within the range of influence of developed political systems, we repeatedly find such higher levels of political unity. Examples can be seen in the American Southeast (where the system is not too well understood by anthropologists), possibly in Polynesia, and widely in Africa. The Baganda on the north shore of Lake Victoria have an economy based on plantains, which provide abundant food on a long-term basis. Since, under favorable conditions, a plantation of these bananas remains productive for thirty years and the labor of a single household with an adequate plot of land can regularly produce more food than its members require, a society using plantains as its staple can maintain a high population density on a permanent basis and also free some people from basic productive activity. At the same time, there is ample reason to believe that the development of a large-scale political system in Buganda was ultimately a product of diffusion from the eastern Mediterranean area.

AGRICULTURAL SOCIETIES

Agriculture with more advanced technology, associated with highly developed political systems, has had three areas of original development: the Near East and western India, Southeast Asia and China, and an area in the Americas extending from Mexico to Chile. Productive techniques, and crops used, are similar within each area, so we prefer to see each as a single general basic development, sharing not only a substratum of similar culture but having some distant but effective communication during the period of their development. In each of these three areas, there were several separate regions of cultural growth and political organization.

Both Old World examples rest upon the use of plow and draft animals; the Far Eastern farming involved wet rice; the Near Eastern irrigated small grains. Crops and techniques both differed. In the New World farming practices did not involve the plow. In Peru terracing and fertilization were more advanced techniques for sustaining large-scale political units. In Mexico high production was achieved on the *chinampas,* the so-called floating gardens which were in reality artificially built islands on which the topsoil was replenished annually. The Maya had no advanced techniques, but the southern portion of this area was highly productive. It is likely that other parts of the New World area of high culture were farmed by slash-and-burn without further technical advances.

Though our viewpoint has been fundamentally that the economic situation renders developments possible and enforces limitations upon them, we must not forget that institutions are also devices for improving man's condition. Political institutions are a case in point; apparently unification and organization, perhaps also the elimination of constant warfare and feuding, can support large and stable populations. Something of the kind appears to have taken place in a good deal of the area of high culture in the Americas.

Once political institutions develop, their impact can be diffused to outlying areas. This clearly happened in European history. Middle American influences apparently reached the southeastern United States. Similar developments in Africa have already been mentioned.

On the other hand, advanced techniques do not always produce political states. We find social atomism comparable to that of simpler horticultural peoples throughout much of the Philippine Islands, for example. High productive capacity must be seen as a necessary but not sufficient basis for the development of large-scale political entities.

Large-scale political systems are delicate social units, especially in their more formative phases, and history provides innumerable examples of their demise. The institu-

tional techniques for the preservation of states are
necessarily elaborate and as a result, states are propor-
tionately friable. Aside from the matter of size, state systems
are vulnerable on two interrelated counts. First, they involve populations of diverse backgrounds and cultural
orientations (as will be discussed below) and therefore
cannot build their sense of unity out of general cultural
assumption but must create the sense of community solidarity by special institutions and propaganda devices. Second,
the generic problem in all social organization, the subordination of individual interest to the public weal, is
aggravated by state organization—in part because of the
cultural diversity just mentioned and in part because of the
concentration of power and decision making. On the other
hand, such political systems have their sources of strength,
particularly against external forces, and because they can
make possible higher levels of living.

Wherever agricultural states are found, there is increased
specialization. Thus far, we have not spoken of the division
of labor beyond that of age and sex, for it has played an
insignificant role in the organization of primitive societies.
The shaman and other religious functionaries are the only
true specialists in most hunting and horticultural societies,
and even these specialists usually take part in the fundamental economic pursuits of the community. Craft special-
ties that emerge out of the differential skills of particular
individuals do not normally free them from basic food
production. Widely in Asia and Africa, the smith provides
the exception, and he is viewed as either very specially
sacred or very specially dangerous—perhaps just because he
is an outsider to the normal activities, practicing a black
art that is clearly the product of civilized invention. But
efficient farming frees many persons from the basic pursuits
because it enables one farm family to feed mouths other
than their own with reasonable stability and in sufficient

quantity. Such persons can pursue their specialty, whether it be craft, priesthood, military, or governance, unhampered by the need to hunt game or till the soil. Their freedom enables them to develop techniques which increase their productive capacity and ultimately to increase the capacity of those who remain on the soil. Such specialists tend to concentrate where they may exchange their services and wares with one another and where the farmers can bring them the necessary sustenance. Thus cities are born.

The coming into being of cities forms a major step in the organization of society, a product of a long evolution with far-reaching consequences. A society with cities inevitably has two ways of life, widely different in character, widely different in activities and expectations, yet dependent upon each other. The farmer comes to expect the goods and services of the city, and the city man gets his sustenance from the farmer.

With the growth of cities, multiple ways of life emerge within a single social system. In order now to speak of social organization, we must necessarily examine three separate units: the city, the peasant or farming community, and the state system as a whole which binds these two together.

The circumstances of urban life, which derive from the fact that cities are constituted of a large, dense aggregate of heterogeneous peoples, have consequences for the character of urban social organization. Many sociologists, notably the German Ferdinand Tönnies and the American Louis Wirth, have written of the characteristic life modes of cities. The size and density means that people who do not know one another are constantly in interaction. That is, there must be means for them to communicate and engage in commerce. Their large number means that each person knows many of his fellow citizens only through limited contacts and most of them not at all—though normally each person will still have kin and associates whom he knows well. It is to this that reference is made when one speaks of the city as being impersonal. In such a situation, external symbols replace entirely the basis of ordinary social evaluation among the citizenry, so that evidence of economic well-being takes a central place in the value system along with (and closely related to) proximity to the seats of power.

The heterogeneity of urban populations is even more significant. This heterogeneity is of two kinds: of cultural background and of current life activities. Cultural heterogeneity rests on a basic and very nearly universal fact of urban life. Historically, and to a considerable extent today, cities do not reproduce themselves. Cities consume the people; the rural areas produce them. For urban birth rate tends to decline relative to death rate. The death rate rises under urban conditions because of the difficulties of sanitation and the characteristics of communicable diseases, which can more easily develop epidemic proportions in city populations. With increased medical knowledge, this tendency has been checked, but that same knowledge has led to better methods of birth control which (coupled with urban economic conditions) has tended to reduce birth rates. This inability of cities to maintain their own populations—and certainly to provide their growth—has meant that at any one time, the city is made up of some people who were born there and of some who, as youths or young adults, moved in from the outside. Thus, at least two cultural backgrounds are represented. And these outsiders themselves come from widely diverse backgrounds. Colonies of foreign residents are found among the earliest archeologically known cities. The development of such agglomerations of population from different cultures and social circumstances was also found in Mexico at the time of the Conquest and has been an ever-increasing part of urban development in Europe since the decline of feudal institutions. In present-day Africa one can see similar patterns, with a strong tendency for peasants to congregate with those of their fellow tribesmen who preceded them to the city.

Urban cultural heterogeneity is further compounded by the fact that city dwellers engage in a variety of occupations: they are specialists living different kinds of life, having different skills, values, and patterns of behavior. Life experiences among urban residents vary in a way that they do not among the residents in tribal societies or peasant communities. In the modern world, it is not easy to know the characteristic life activities of a person whose occupation is different from one's own and often seems mysterious. In crafts and professions there are special values and symbols of achievement which give the craftsman or practitioner satisfaction. But such achievements are rarely known to his associates beyond the immediate family and the workers in his own field.

This dual heterogeneity, which is characteristic of all urban situations in greater or lesser degree, and which is absent from all tribal societies, has profound effects on social life. It is, perhaps, the only true intellectual justification for the separation of anthropology from sociology (though there are practical and historic reasons for the separation). Such heterogeneity means that society can no longer operate in terms of cultural assumptions; that is, the assumption that a normal person will act in certain specified ways. Instead, it must provide laws and law-enforcing machinery to preserve the society itself, rather than to protect one individual or group from another. It cannot assume that people will share a common set of values. Instead, the variant values of divergent groups are trans-

lated into the common denominator of money or other
form of wealth. Status systems tend to be related directly to
wealth or proximity to the seats of power.

The spatial groups, such as bands and villages, and the
kinship groups, such as clans, lose importance in urban
social life. This is not to say that proximity or kinship disappear as factors of social life, but only that they become
subordinate to groups defined on economic, ethnic, and
social bases. We remember from European history the important part that guilds played during the emergence of
cities in the Middle Ages. Similar craft-oriented social
units appeared repeatedly in the early Eastern cities, among
the Aztecs, and among the Baganda of East Africa. Such
crafts and guilds are not infrequently based upon a common ethnic background: people from the same region enter
the same type of trade, either because it fits in with their
subcultural background, or because old ethnic ties provide
entree into the occupational activity. The former is exemplified by Toro potters who continue in modern Uganda
to form an ethnic enclave of common occupation in
Kampala; the latter is reported for emergent cities in West
Africa.

Occupation and ethnic background are, therefore, closely
associated with wealth and power and are often major
determinants of social status in urban life and form the
basis for a system of social classes. Such social classes are
not merely occupation groups but are sectors of the population who enjoy or suffer different life modes and who
have different degrees of prestige and power. They frequently are greatly divergent in economic circumstances.
For, with the cultural heterogeneity and the occupational
variety of urban populations, values become increasingly
depersonalized and status rests more and more on economic
considerations. It is a rule of economics that one can add
apples and oranges only by translating each into its eco-

nomic value, and this applies also to the social evaluation of urban residents. The result is a proliferation of physical symbols of status, especially in the form of housing, dress, and personal adornment, in the evident opportunities to enjoy leisure, and in the command of personal services. A recurrent element in all urban civilization has been the creation of sumptuary regulations which give the force of law to these criteria of social differentiation. Such social differentiation, coupled with the inevitable trend toward preserving one's current status *in perpetuum* through one's offspring, gives rise to permanent social classes, which often are actually different subcultures. Such social discrimination appears in the urban environments in primitive state systems, even as in the ancient Greek and late Aztec, where some democratic institutions prevailed.

Meanwhile the peasant communities remain. The village dweller is still a farmer; as in primitive societies, the whole rural population engages in the same occupation and shares a common set of values. It is no wonder that much literature on folk communities lumps them together with the more primitive systems of hunting and food-gathering and horticulture. The more naturally so, because the folk community tends to be traditional and conservative in outlook, adhering to old ways of doing things and old patterns of thought.

But the folk society is quite different from tribal society and these differences must be appreciated. We define a folk society as a geographically delimited community operating within the framework of a state organization. A mosaic of such communities covers the land within the orbit of a political system. The peasants in each village live largely within it, tied to sister villages only through loyalty or subjugation to the common political entity. Though the difference between tribe and peasant community may seem a small one, the consequences of a tie to a national state are far-reaching. Consider first that the folk community normally lives in an enforced peace (for war is the prerogative of the state); its boundaries are set; it cannot act against its neighboring community to expand when it grows large and strong but must live within the resources available to it. Since it lives on a fixed amount of land, it rapidly presses on these resources. Normally, the citizenry of a peasant community is impoverished. For this reason, and because sustenance comes from farming, land is central to the value system and the ownership of or a right to land is tantamount to citizenship in the community. All social institutions and values revolve around landholding, which forever remains the core of the social organization of the typical folk community.

Another element that sets off the peasant village from the tribal community is that, whereas the village is homogeneous in occupation and culture, it nevertheless lives in the context of an alien and alternate cultural system. Urban values do insinuate themselves into the folk community and heterogeneity is present in concept even when it is not in experience. This is different from the knowledge that one tribe may have of its neighbor's divergent culture, for here the two are separate systems; in the folk community, however, the alien system is joined to it and is even superordinate. Folk values and folk culture must take cognizance of these urban influences, if only by the elaborate denial of urban values, while subtly being seduced into such elements of urban behavior as the peasant can afford. From an analysis of Mexican folk societies, George Foster concludes that most of peasant culture derives from the city, but from times past.

Urban culture and social values are often forced upon the folk community. The peasant comes to rely on urban technology, trading his foods for the products of the city craftsman. He is subject to urban control, usually in the form of military service and taxes, subject to its juridical system, and to both sacred and secular administration.

So the peasant population, living in the rural areas, has a social organization different from that of its urban fellow citizens, but not uninfluenced by their existence. This social system is the true folk community. We may presume that early in the development of states, or more recently where state systems have covered an area and incorporated an existing population, the patterns of behavior and the social organization of the peasant community were built on its pre-existing cultural mode of living. Such is implicit for the Old World in antiquity and perhaps for much of the New World in prehistoric times. As we observe the Buganda kingdom and the folk culture of its hinterland, we feel strongly the continuation of old tribal customs in the contemporary folk community. No doubt elsewhere there has been a more synthetic pattern of development of folk communities—as for example in the more "backward" areas of America, such as James West described in *Plainville, U.S.A.* This Ozark town, made up of Americans with ultimate European background, had developed a strong sense of its local integrity, had a host of folk customs, and a system of social organizations not unlike folk communities in Europe or Asia. We presume that this is an unusual pattern, yet in Egypt, Europe, and much of Asia, the folk community is of such antiquity that it may have gone through untold changes.

However the folk community came into existence, it tends rapidly to develop characteristic features of social organization that are in keeping with the conditions of life imposed upon it by its encapsulation within the state. Central to this organization are two major interrelated elements: land and family. Land is, of course, the basis of subsistence, but it is far more. Land is always central to the value system; the distinction between landholders and the landless separates true citizens from something less than citizens, and the size of holdings is closely related to social status. Associated with the land are its appurtenances such as tools and stock; thus the quality of husbandry may also become central in the value system. To hold land, to use it well, to increase it, are prime motivations in the typical peasant society.

But as men are mortal while agricultural land continues its value in perpetuity, there inevitably arises the problem of continuity of this primary value. This in part accounts for the strong sense of family solidarity, for the family shares an interest in the land. The family head often merely holds the land for the family, which continues through time. The peasant family usually has these features: it is patrilineal and patrilocal and family solidarity continues through the generations, so that filial relations are more important than marital ones. Children are highly desired, particularly sons. And the whole set-up is heavily sanctioned by religious beliefs.

The patriliny of peasant families is associated with the fact that men almost always are in charge of farming in peasant societies. This probably derives from the fact that the circumstances of folk life deprive men of their earlier economic pursuits: war and hunting. For war (with few exceptions) is not a regular occupation of the peasants or the road to glory, and dense settlements make game scarce and hunting the sport of the privileged.

The strong emphasis upon consanguinous ties is a means of continuing family holdings. Three-generation families, with adult sons working for the father on the family land, are recurrent. In such a case, marriage is frequently viewed as a family matter, not an individual one, and continued service to the land is more important than the quixotic and transient satisfactions of romantic love. Hence in China a marriage is viewed more as the acquisition of a daughter-

in-law than of a wife. This was true also in the ancient
Mediterranean world. Associated with this is the emphasis
upon having children—particularly sons—without which
the family and its holding could not continue. This emphasis makes for a high birth rate in folk communities and
compounds the difficulties attendant upon the scarcity of
land and the pressures of population. Thus we meet the
paradox of the strong demand for children to meet cultural values in the face of economic stress and want.

The desire for children regularly poses a problem: how
to pass on the land. To this there is no satisfactory solution,
and almost every possible one can be exemplified: primo-
geniture, ultimogeniture, equal division among all sons,
equal division among all children. Each has its virtues and
its difficulties. Whatever the solution, however, two features generally follow. First, there is some means of holding
family lands together, and second, there is a need for emi-
gration from rural areas. It is these emigrants who supply
the population to the cities. Meanwhile, the family system
is supported not only by traditional values, but also by
religious institutions which sanction family solidarity and
strengthen its essential features.

The third element in societies at the level of developed
agriculture is the state as a whole. A state may be said to
exist when a recognized system of central authority ad-
ministers a broad territory of separate communities. The
administration is located in an urban center. A true state
properly involves a panoply of functions which provide for
the continuity of an organized system, including: (1) a seat
of authority with clear provisions for the transmission of
office; (2) a system of administration reaching out to the
local citizenry; (3) a means of supporting the authority
system through a form of police; (4) a system of adjudication whereby disputes are handled by the state rather than
by the direct action of feud; (5) a unified religious system

which gives ideological sanction to the system of authority; (6) a military to protect the integrity of the state against outside enemies—often, of course, through aggression—and; (7) a system of commerce which enables the regular exchange of goods between urban and rural dwellers and among the specialists of the urban center. Most political states show all these features.

When political systems emerge—what we have here called primitive state systems—there is a remarkable degree of similarity in their social institutions. These similarities of institutions and their development were pointed out some ten years ago in a paper by the American anthropologist, Julian Steward. He compared the developmental phases in northern Peru, Mesoamerica, Mesopotamia, Egypt, and China. In these five cradles of civilization, he believes, the "exploitation [of the environment] by a pre-metal technology seems to have entailed similar solutions to similar problems and consequently to have caused similar developmental sequences." Steward is concerned with laws of growth and development; here we wish to focus on institutional similarities. Most primitive state systems share these features: high concentration of power in the hands of an individual; sanction of power with some kind of theocratic ideology; a priesthood, usually highly elaborated, which is itself powerful and makes the theocratic ideology tangible to the population; hereditary nobility which gives secular support to the center of power and usually is in charge of the military; a system of social classes including a slave class, and a separate artisan group as well as the nobility; a means of controlling commerce, either through controlled (and often taxed) markets or through a monetary system; a strong military, organized for aggressive warfare; a system of roads to make communication possible, usually fanning out from the seat of power; sumptuary regulations that give the force of law to social distinctions and the public expression of prestige; values in leisure, noneconomic activities, and elaborate ornamentation (and hence of the arts), and in military exploits.

Such parallels derive from the functional demands and the evolutionary process. That state systems are delicate, especially in their initial stages, has already been noted. It seems likely that most or all of these features (and undoubtedly others as well) are requisite in order to preserve a state system. For, at the primitive level of statehood, the advantages of national organization are far from self-evident to the rank and file, and the institutional means for control over the people and for developing national loyalties are necessary. When, however, technologies advance, so that urban manufactured goods increase the life circumstances of the population as a whole, as is the case of modern life, then the commitment to large political entities is complete. One may get changes of personnel, but not the destruction of the system.

HERDING SOCIETIES

Herding societies are those in which the people's lives are dominated by the requirements of the livestock they keep, from which they obtain their major sustenance. It involves keeping domestic animals, but not all people with livestock are to be considered herders. The Kazaks of Central Asia, the Bedouins of Arabia, and the Masai of East Africa are good examples of herding peoples. Where herding is found, the land and climate are not favorable to farming with the techniques known in the area (though with large-scale construction and modern power equipment, it may be quite productive, as is demonstrated in Israel today). Usually aridity is the limiting factor, though in the far north, agriculture is prevented by other aspects of climate. The environment provides shrubs or grass that sheep, goats, cattle, horses, and other animals can eat and thereby convert into food amenable to human consumption. Man can thereby utilize such arid areas. To do so, he must order his own life to the needs of his animals— moving them to new pastures, sheltering them in winter, seeking water during the dry season. Such a territory can sustain a larger population of herders than it could of hunters, but the population is relatively sparse, and must remain mobile. For this reason herding peoples have social systems on the general level of the horticulturalists in terms of population and organizational requirements, though the mode of life makes for many specific differences.

One might naturally presume that herding peoples emerge directly from hunting. It seems reasonable to assume that game hunters might husband their quarry and reduce them to flocks and herds, and this assumption is given further credence by the external similarities between a nomadic herding life and that of the nomadic hunters. Apparently, however, this was not the case. Domestication of animals, according to the available archeological evidence, appears to have taken place first among horticultural and agricultural peoples. It is assumed that the first flocks were developed on the stubble fields of grain farmers. If this evidence is correct, then herding is a quite late adjustment: an ecologically determined devolution to a simpler mode of life.

In one sense, herding has developed independently several times, and in another sense it has not. The evidence from the plains of America suggests that the Indians picked up very little knowledge of the horse from the Spanish, and they certainly made their own adaptation of its use; yet clearly it was the Spanish who provided the idea of domestication and riding. The Hottentots probably also developed their use of cattle independently, in the sense that they never saw true arid-land herding, yet presumably they obtained cattle from the Bantu who got them, in turn, from herders to the north. On the other hand, peoples of the Asiatic tundra apparently learned the notion of herding from cattle- and horse-trading peoples and applied it to the reindeer which they themselves domesticated. Herding as a mode of life also developed after the discovery of America on the South American pampas and in the southwestern United States, where it has become the primary mode of livelihood of the Navaho and other tribes. Though a large part of the globe is covered by herding peoples and herding is now found on all continents, there appears to be a historic continuity from a single origin. Llamas and alpacas were domesticated in South America, but there is no evidence of an independent herding culture.

Herding societies generally operate in units of several hundred people who move about together over a wide area. Apparently there is an optimal size of herd unit for various animals and environments, and this size requires the co-operative effort of a number of persons. The size of human groups, as well as of the herds, and the patterns of ownership vary. The kind of animal is a factor in such variation, for large animals, such as cattle, have different needs than small animals, such as sheep. The environment can vary from true desert, such as the Sahara or the Sinai Peninsula, to semiarid country, and to tundra for reindeer herding.

Lush country generally turns to farming, which is then the more rewarding life mode, and so does land which can be irrigated. The economic arrangements also vary. Some herders live almost entirely off their stock, as do the Masai of East Africa. Some live largely by engaging in trade, as do many camel keepers in North Africa and some of the Mongol tribes. Others have a variety of relationships with farmers or farming: the Navahos engage in small-scale horticulture as a side line; the Watutsi of Ruanda-Urundi in central Africa, and the Tuareg of the Sahara have subordinated a horticulturist class, from which they obtain agricultural products. Others have traded with or plundered urban settlements. The New World developments of horse herding on the plains and pampas involved the use of domestic animals for the hunting of game, rather than directly as food.

In addition to these arrangements in which herding tribes remain separate, and in which farming is entirely incidental or is carried out by a subordinate class, the keeping of livestock may be more closely associated with either horticulture or agriculture. Dairying throughout Europe is a major activity, but dairy cows are fed from cultivated fields and kept in enclosed pastures. The dairyman is chiefly farmer, even though he may seasonally pasture his herd. Cattle keeping is an important adjunct to the horticultural life throughout central and southern Africa, wherever there is freedom from the tsetse fly. Such peoples have a dual way of life; often the men are virtually herders while the women are horticulturists. Economic, climatologic, and historic factors have made for various amalgamations. Here, however, we are concerned with the relatively pure forms of nomadic herders.

The analysis of the social organization of Asiatic, African, and old European herding societies by the American anthropologist Elizabeth Bacon indicates a high degree of uniformity. She found that throughout most of the Old World the herding societies are organized on a consistent basic pattern which Africanists have called segmented lineages but for which she suggests the Mongol term *Obok*. The Obok is like a clan in that it is an extension of familism including a broad sector of relatives, but its principles of organization differ. These segmented lineages are built upon a genealogic principle, so that a broad one (often encompassing a whole tribe) recognizes a common ancestor; within it are contained a series of subdivisions, and within these again further divisions, and so on, until one comes down to the local bands of a few families.

Each group has its own land. It also has limited rights to the land of the more inclusive units of which it is a part, the whole being tied together by the fiction of common ancestors and governed basically on kinship principles. The pattern is more flexible than that of true clans, and perhaps this flexibility is particularly important for adjustment to the variant conditions of herding and the need for movement. The units tend to be patrilineal and patrilocal, and women generally become part of their husbands' Obok (in contrast to clans, where each person remains forever in his natal clan). They are not infrequently endogamic; at least they allow marriages within the group, as long as the kinship is not closer than cousin. Though not every herding group has this system, it is extremely widespread in the Old World; and although it probably has a single historic origin, it must have particular value for societies in which the economy is based on the maintenance of animals, since it has such a long continuity, wide distribution, and close association with herding.

Certain other features are widespread, if not universal. First, the animals themselves are always central in the value system. The ownership of stock is not merely important for its economic usefulness but is an end in itself, and numbers are more important than quality. The situation is quite comparable to ownership of land among the peasants. Second, land among herders is generally treated as a free good, and where farmers coexist, it is frequently their responsibility to maintain fences. A kind of herding society emerged on the Great Plains after the Civil War, diffusing out of Texas, and the basic epic of the West is the hostility between these herders and the settlers; their major cause for bloodshed was fences. Tradition, established law, and economic forces combined to settle the issue over most of this area, but on the arid and mountainous public lands of the intermontane region of the United States, herding is still practiced, and the rights of cattlemen and sheepmen to use of the land is recognized, though they must officially obtain permits.

Third, livestock is always translatable into other goods, notably, almost always used in exchange for wives, so that the herd has an important bearing on the more personal aspects of well-being, and sexual satisfaction (and the prestige of multiple wives) comes to be directly related to the availability of livestock. Similarly, livestock is central to the power relationships, and the holding of large herds is frequently the basis for the large social aggregates with the head as nominal owner of the herd and controlling power of his familistic social entity. Hence a special extension of family organization centers around the herds—units which are frequently massive in size.

Finally, livestock is a particular kind of wealth subject to particular conditions. The husbandry of animals requires hard and rough work of the kind most characteristically engaged in by men, presumably because of their average superior strength. Herding is therefore predominantly a masculine operation and rare, indeed, is the true herding society which is not patrilineal and male-centered. Stock is a volatile kind of wealth, and unforeseen circumstances—climate, disease, predatory animals, and hostile neighbors—may decimate herds in a single season. For this reason there may be a relatively large amount of social mobility in herding societies. There are also elaborate institutional devices to protect the wealth and power of herd owners. Presumably this is a reason for the recurrent tendency to emphasize numbers of livestock rather than quality, even at the cost of long-term efficiency. We have here a situation not unlike that of the peasant desire for children: the herder values his stock and derives prestige from having large numbers of them; the numbers in turn tend to destroy the resource base on which they live. Thus cultural values are in conflict with long-term economic stability. The hazardous nature of herding operations and the social mobility it engenders contribute to another recurrent characteristic of herders: a fierce independence and a militaristic-aggressive character.

We should take special note of the Indians of the Great Plains of North America. Prior to discovery by the white men, this area was divided between horticultural tribes in the east and hunting and food-gathering peoples in the west, both operating under poor circumstances. The introduction of the horse created a new ecological opportunity for the Indians, who moved in from all sides and developed a herding economy based on the horse, altering their institutions to meet these new circumstances. The history of the Plains is the prime example of ecological adaptation, but the opportunity for a final pattern to emerge was never fulfilled because new factors (traders, guns, settlers) were continuously introduced and constantly altered the balance of power and the character of opportunity. It was also a unique development since the horses were not themselves a source of sustenance but rather the means by which bison could be efficiently exploited. Nevertheless, the major elements of a herding system were clearly emerging, for, after all, horses were the capital goods by means of which the livelihood was obtained. The degree to which the cultural modes of these Indians were adapted to the herding way of life was demonstrated by a chance experiment: the Canadian government's efforts to provide for a self-contained economy for the Blackfoot Indians, after the periods of trapping and furnishing horses to European packers came to a close. It tried to induce the Blackfoot to engage in farming, but this effort failed, because the life modes were too different and land per se had no meaning to the Blackfoot. When, however, they started them on range cattle, the Blackfoot economy and the whole social outlook improved.

INDUSTRIAL SOCIETIES

A new mode of economy has entered the picture, but it is so recent and so developmental that we cannot know what ultimate patterns of organizational needs will emerge. This economy is the industrial, wherein production utilizes chemical and physical rather than human and animal energy.

The most obvious emerging element in this new social order is the high degree of specialization and the increasing importance of elaborate systems of exchange. For this reason the nature of the specialization (i.e., occupation) tends to determine the primary life modes of the individual and also his social status. The society tends to become atomistic; the justification of social behavior rests less upon traditional than upon rationalized means : ends assumptions. This is not to say that industrial society becomes a Brave New World, for the old demands of sexual and social needs remain. Man continues to operate within a constellation of family organizations (though family decreases in importance relative to other social groups) and people continue to be mutually interdependent.

Society increasingly partakes of the urban characteristics, unleavened by a peasant hinterland. This has already gone far in the United States, and parts of Western Europe; and where industrial farming dominates the countryside (as in California and the American Southwest) it has gone so far that the social patterns of rural communities are essentially the same as those of urban centers.

Meanwhile, unlimited sources of power make unprecedentedly high standards of living possible for the masses, giving leisure and mobility to individuals of moderate means. With such universal wealth available, status based upon property may well decline and a re-emergence of preferred types of activity may come to dominate the value system—furthered by the fact that control of knowledge rather than of resources will be crucial to the economy. We have only just begun to see the age of the specialist.

PROBLEMS INHERENT IN SOCIAL TAXONOMY

We have tried to express the central features of the major taxonomic category as they generally appear, without suggesting that each is internally uniform or that bold exceptions never occur. Indeed, our evolutionary hypothesis denies inevitability; it rather asserts central tendencies. For the forces at work on the character of social institutions are sociological, and the sociological fulfillment of these imperatives is subject to secondary and often fortuitous circumstances. For example, we would assert that a population protected from outside influences by barriers against aggression may very well continue with institutional devices that could not be maintained if there were better organized societies in the area. Examples recur at many places. The lack of social solidarity and institutional unity among the Havasupai Indians, in their deep gorge near the Grand Canyon in northwestern Arizona, may continue just because they are protected by their environment. Again, the highly atomistic patterns on the New Guinea highlands—where each village seems to be the enemy of every other—would not long remain were the area readily subjected to invasion by outside groups with superior organizational devices. Their protection is best demonstrated by the fact that the area was only discovered to modern society in 1931.

Again, we must not lose sight of the fact that we are dealing with the broad basis by which the society fulfills the social imperatives, not with the details of culture. The animal pelts which serve as prestige symbols vary between the Indians of central California (bear hides) and northwestern California (skins of albino deer), but in each case they serve as symbols of status and as goads to action; and each is consonant with the capacities and limitations of a settled hunting and food-gathering society. The uniformities we discuss are broad functional ones, not details of form and aspect. Just how detailed the similarities may ultimately be found to be will rest upon more elaborate analysis and sharper taxonomy.

Finally, in social and cultural matters, each entity does not and cannot remain pure in type. We have noted cases where one economic form under special environmental circumstances takes on the characteristics of a more advanced one, and have seen examples of mixed economic types, such as the African peoples who combine herding and horticulture and have a social organization that takes on some characteristics of each type of economy. The diffusion of cultural elements from one people to another and the integration of variant elements makes for mixed systems.

Ethnographic literature provides information about a wide range of social systems. Yet with all these strictures and words of caution the classification yields us a first approximation, and it illuminates a good deal both of the broad sweep of human history, and the forces that shape human behavior and cultural forms.

VII

The Scientific Study of Society

H UMAN SOCIETY has been viewed in this book as a system of interpersonal relationships. These operate in
a real world made up on the one hand of the needs and
capacities of its human components, and on the other of
the recalcitrant elements of an environment, out of which
these needs are supplied. This is neither biological nor
environmental determinism, for the significant elements in
our analysis are social and cultural. Yet the social and cultural needs are limited and channeled by these elements
which are external to the system.

For purposes of our analysis, the focal point is man's
commitment to social existence, a commitment that is
perduring and inexorable, and in terms of which all further elements of social behavior are to be seen. It is an
old assumption, having variously been expressed as man's
being a political animal or being possessed of a social
instinct akin to the instinct of bees. While endeavoring
to avoid such biological terminology, we have nevertheless
found it necessary to predicate that this commitment lies
behind culture; that it is a tendency in man (however he
has come by it) which is outside the cultural system and
everywhere present. To consider it a product of culture

and then proceed to explain cultural behavior in terms of it is a narrow circle of argument. We have spoken of this commitment as a human need, the need for positive affect, and we postulate that this quest is central in human behavior, drawing men everywhere into the vortex of the demands their cultural environment makes of them, rendering them willing to submit to the hardships and indignities that such cultural life often imposes. Clinical psychology gives support to this viewpoint, but we readily admit that there, too, it is only a postulate and not a demonstrable fact.

Man's commitment to society and his need for positive affect can be seen as a two-edged sword. No claim is made for a predominant urge to love; rather, man is seen as self-seeking. But his efforts to meet his selfish interests cannot operate except in the context of others through whom his personal satisfaction may be had. Society is the recurrent, the inevitable answer. And society must be organized to balance off the pull of individual self-seeking against the demands of social harmony.

This leads to the first of the two central themes of this book: that the formulation and preservation of society requires certain features called the *social imperatives*. It is our contention that if a community is long to survive, these elements must exist, that they are requisite for that balance between personal goals and social commitment just mentioned. They might have been called sociological laws, but they are not formulated in terms of scientific law and do not have quite the quality implicit in the phrase. We call them imperatives and use the word *must*. But the imperative and the must are conditional in that there is no ultimate demand that either man or society need continue to exist, but only that they are necessary if the society is to continue.

The various ways in which these imperatives are met

depend upon the circumstances of the society, and although these circumstances may vary in many ways, there is one major kind of orderliness in that variation: evolutionary development. This has been our second major thesis. Evolution of man's practical knowledge proceeds by an internal logic based upon man's rational efforts to meet his needs. However imperfectly that development has proceeded in time, however variant and disparate and impeded by folly or pigheadedness it has been (for man does not always use his capacity for rational action), the broad sweep of human history shows a gradually increasing mastery over man's material requirements. This we treat as an independent variable, subject largely (but not entirely) to its self-contained inner dynamic. What interests us as students of social behavior is the dependent variable, the character of the social system which is a concomitant of this technological growth. For although man has sufficient ingenuity to develop a wide variety of specific modes for meeting the imperative elements of social systems, broad general uniformities do appear at various levels of technical proficiency.

We offer them here as a first approximation in the belief that the comparative analysis of social behavior requires a broad system of generalization within which more specific uniformities and regularities may be examined. Anthropologists have avoided such systems, dissuaded by the exuberance of early theorists. Sociologists are deprived of them by the heavy concentration of their attention on one end of the range of social variability—modern industrial society. (To be sure, they have asserted it implicitly, for the recurrent theory of urban life reiterated by Emile Durkheim, Ferdinand Tönnies, Louis Wirth, and others is an assertion that conditions deriving from technology create circumstances that require recurrent social solutions irrespective of cultural orientation.)

This book has centered its thesis on two aspects of anthropological theory, but it is important to realize that it does not involve the denial of any of anthropology's major orientations. As discussed in an earlier chapter, the various sources of explanation do not, in fact, conflict. They involve, rather, the diverse factors operating on human beings. We can go further and state that any theory dealing with human social systems requires the integration of such divergent orientations. Our thesis here has not only recognized the validity of alternative orientations but is actually built on the assumption that the sociological and evolutionary constructs require one another.

We note that the better evolutionary writers, such as Sir Henry Maine and Lewis Henry Morgan, also saw this evolution in a sociological, i.e., a functional, sense, for the working out of the character of society at various levels involves assumptions of functional interrelationships. Although our discussion focuses on only these two orientations, we have nowhere denied the psychodynamics of cultural involvement or the implications of historical continuity and cultural diffusion. A more detailed treatment of the relationship between the postulated need for positive affect and the character of value orientations would certainly require elaboration of the psychological mechanisms involved.

Man does not each time invent for himself when he is culturally ready; the accidents of time and place, of isolation and contiguity, are pertinent to the understanding of the human scene. History is involved. But the fact that human events are unique does not disprove the possibility of regularity in human social behavior. Indeed, the question as to whether or not history repeats itself can be quite simply resolved by the distinction between events and phenomena. An *event* is a particular occurrence in time and space, such as might be reported in an ethnography or history. The storming of the Bastille and the Boston Tea Party were events in human history, each occurring but once. Each, however, was a denial of authority when the value system no longer gave legitimacy to that authority, and each was an act calculated to rally the community to new values. They may therefore be considered a single phenomenon. A *phenomenon* is thus a sociological generalization of which the specific acts are examples, just as *Pinus ponderosa* is a generalization about a host of similar though not identical pine trees. The assumption underlying social science is that phenomena do repeat themselves.

Useful scientific generalization requires both a taxonomy of events and a theory of relevance. Anthropology has too much avoided both. Early evolutionary theory provided anthropology with a classification of societies on a hierarchical level of development. The rejection of this schema led to the tendency to lump together all peoples outside Western civilization under the term *primitives*. Actually, this came to include all those people who were normally the subject of anthropological inquiry. The Aztecs and the Incas were in (since we knew them largely by means of archeology), but the Greeks and Romans were out (because they were early the province of history and classics). The result was that massive African and Southeast Asiatic kingdoms enter into our theories along with, and taxonomically (and therefore conceptually) undifferentiated from, the Arunta and the Andaman Islanders. Consider, for instance, Paul Radin's classic and creative *Primitive Man as Philosopher,* which includes references to many peoples (provided they lack writing) or the only broad contemporary analysis of economic life by Melville Herskovits, *The Economic Life of Primitive People,* as its first edition was called. In neither instance does the author regularly investigate whether the elements of his analysis

vary with different kinds of primitive peoples—different
in evolutionary stages or according to any other relevant
criteria.

The underlying rationale of this procedure is that after
all, human beings are all really alike. This statement is true
only when the "really" refers to man's innate average capacities and needs; and as far as this is true, it renders the
distinction between *primitives* (i.e., the usual subject of
anthropological inquiry) and *moderns* (i.e., the usual subject of sociological inquiry) entirely useless as well. Actually, of course, the subject of our study is not man as such,
but aspects of his culture and his social institutions. And
these, quite clearly, are not alike. Nor is it any more appropriate to lump the Ashanti with the Arunta than to
lump them with modern Americans. To me, it seems much
less appropriate. The discomfort in the procedure has been
demonstrated by those who engage in it, for they have
placed a tabu on the word *primitive* (though it is too useful to be entirely avoided). The circumlocutions that have
developed, words such as *preliterate* or *nonliterate,* do not
resolve the problem because they avoid the true issue,
which is the rejection of efforts to categorize into significant
entities the broad and disparate phenomena that are the
socieites with which anthropologists deal. In the final
analysis, *primitive* is a comparative rather than an absolute
word, and by any reasonable use of it, the Arunta are more
primitive than the Ashanti, the Ashanti more than modern
Americans. It must again be emphasized that the term has
no reference to virtue or morality or to the intellectual
capacites of the peoples involved; it is a statement of the
condition of their technical apparatus and the social institutions. *Good* and *bad* are terms properly left to the philos-
ophers; *simple* and *complex, primitive* and *advanced* are
crass but useful scientific expressions.

This leads us to face the problem of cultural relativity

and the evaluation of social systems, as any treatise on comparative society should. The dominant mode of anthropological thought has been relativistic. This seems to stem from the essentially liberal tradition out of which anthropology has grown, a tradition which recognizes human worth in whatever circumstances it is found. In part it is a rejection of the bigotry and cupidity that has characterized, until recently at least, the public attitude toward native peoples, and it specifically expresses a desire to protect these subordinated populations from the discrimination and plundering of a dominant people. It stems in part, too, from a love of the exotic and not a little from the antiquarian interests that drew so many of its practitioners to the anthropological arts. In great measure, it stems from the generic affection and respect that most of us have felt for the natives we meet in the field. Finally, of course, it stems from the fact that as reporters of behavior our descriptions must not be apperceived—in so far as possible—by our prejudices.

In naïve form, cultural relativism asserts that all peoples, all cultures, are equally good: if they be cannibals, well, that's not for me, but *de gustibus*. . . . In more sophisticated form it asserts that each culture must be valued in its own terms: does it satisfy the people themselves? If they are cannibals, what satisfactions does eating human flesh supply in terms of native values? There is much to be said for this point of view; the evaluation of infanticide in the Arctic or the eating of grubs by the Arunta cannot be judged through the love (or ambivalence) we feel toward our children or by our culinary predilections. For this is a judgment of good versus bad, and the good is defined in terms of the conditioning that each of us has had, in terms of our own cultural values.

The problem, however, is not that evaluation is wrong, but, rather, that the basis of evaluation is faulty. It was precisely here that early evolutionists were wrong; they were freely comparing against their own cultural standards. What we need to seek, therefore, is a standard of judgment which is not a product of our own culture. Actually there is but one which is entirely culture-free, but there may be others of sufficient breadth to be useful. That one, of course, is survival value. The history of life itself is predicated on the assumption that life, whether sweet or not, is desirable; desirable not merely for the individual but for the group of which he is a part. The evaluation of cultural behavior then must be made in relation to its viability; and it must be made in terms of the adequacy for continued existence, rather than in terms of moral value or ethical good. (Of course we can—and frequently do—judge some cultures as good and bad because we like or dislike them; but this is frankly a different kind of judgment.)

Underlying such a view is the assumption that social forms are instrumentalities—i.e., that they serve a purpose for life continuation of the group. In an earlier chapter we asserted that the techniques of a culture are instrumentalities that carry the basis for their own evaluation, inasmuch as the technical apparatus is used for specific recognized ends. Institutions, on the other hand, do not have this built-in evaluation. Now, however, we must point out that this is not because they are not actually end-oriented. Rather, it is because the persons in a culture cannot ordinarily view them as such. As social analysts we may note that the flag serves as a symbol of national unity and acts as a reminder and a stimulus to patriotic behavior. So, too, do the totem poles of the Northwest Coast. Both are institutional instrumentalities for the promotion of social cohesiveness. But neither we nor the Tlingit think of the flag or the raven crest as an instrumentality in the sense that we think of the U.S.S. *Nautilus* or a sinew-backed bow. Those living in a culture can make judgments about the physical instrumentality that they cannot make about the social one.

Time, however (and perhaps social analysts), can make different evaluations. Those who participate in a culture may not be perturbed by the inadequacies of its institutions to provide a coherent and viable mode of life. Nero is not the only one to have fiddled while a way of life was being destroyed. Yet in the long run, a social system cannot survive if its institutions for cohesion, order, and the maintenance of physical needs are not met. Here lies the essential dynamic for social evolution and the essential basis for evaluating cultures. If institutions are instrumentalities, they are in fact subject to evaluation.

Thus, we again turn to the evolutionary and functional points of view, for an institution may be a fit instrumentality under one set of circumstances and not under another. Consider here our discussion of clans, which we see as a satisfactory solution to the integrative needs of a stable population at a moderate level of density. The clan systems appear rather too cumbersome at lower levels and quite inadequate at higher ones, so that their functional importance tends to be lost even where clans continue to exist. If we are to evaluate cultural behavior, the evaluation must not only be divested of our own cultural predilections, it must also be in terms of the needs deriving from particular circumstances.

Let us observe this through a favorite anthropological example: Eskimo infanticide. Cultural assumptions in our society place a great premium on the preservation of human life so that we find such a practice repugnant. But Eskimo infanticide is a necessary institution to protect the group, for the proportion of infants to adults in each social unit cannot rise too high. As an instrumentality, it is a useful pattern of behavior even though the people them-

selves might very much prefer other forms of action despite their cultural conditioning. Significantly, the pattern
also appears in desert areas where similar economic conditions prevail. Primitive communism is another example.
All the more sparsely populated hunters and food-gatherers
share the land, and all, I believe, have institutions for
sharing the kill. We cannot see how such institutions could
be avoided at the margins of subsistence, but the recurrence of this phenomenon at such a level is entirely beside
the point in any effort to justify communistic institutions
at any other.

Adequate social institutions do not grow of themselves,
however much they appear to, but must first be conceived
in the minds of men and promulgated by them. They are
not the product of a tropism; they do not develop out
of some sure instinct, such as determines the status hierarchy or the proportion of workers in a colony of bees.
To be sure, sapient beings can foretell consequences and
can seek to avoid those that they fear as harmful—to the
degree that habit and cultural conditioning have not
blinded them. Therefore, it is only in the selective processes, only in the crucible of time, that the fitness of an
institution or a cultural pattern can be tested. Unfortunately, like all clinical tests, these can never provide a
sure answer. No group of American historians can long
converse without raising the question as to what might
have happened had Lincoln not been elected, had the Civil
War not occurred, and so on. Or again, was social security
legislation a product of the New Deal, or was it a necessary
institution forced upon a public by circumstances of an
industrial society awakened by the disaster of 1929?

The answer is equivocal. Circumstances do create needs,
but the needs may be variously met. Even where old conditions manifestly cannot prevail, new solutions are not
necessarily sought, nor are the solutions sought necessarily

adequate. But because people can act instrumentally, they can preserve a situation. This is not only true of modern societies but of primitive ones as well. The case of the Cheyenne Indian named Wolf Lies Down that we examined offered an example of a new regulation being formulated to meet the exigencies of a new situation.

Two anthropologists, John Adair and Evon Vogt, had the opportunity of examining the attitudes of Zuñi and Navaho toward returned veterans of World War II. At Zuñi these men were viewed as a threat to the social order, and through such informal pressures as ridicule and gossip were forced to give up white patterns and return to Zuñi ways. It was a conscious technique on the part of the political and religious leaders to preserve their culture and the integrity of their community. The Navaho were not subjected to this treatment; indeed, they were welcomed as returned warriors and attained a considerable degree of leadership. While several cultural factors and other circumstances are involved, it is clear that Zuñi leadership saw a threat to a way of life and conscientiously took action to ward it off.

Yet for one reason or another, people cannot always act nor can they foresee all the consequences for the future of their present actions. Where institutional adjustment is lacking, the society falls apart or disappears. We can only wonder how many hunting and food-gathering peoples may have perished because they did not develop customs such as sharing and infanticide. We can only wonder whether social systems were engulfed or destroyed by their neighbors because they lacked the integrative devices necessary to protect themselves. We do know that throughout recorded history nations have disappeared because of inadequate institutions to protect their integrity and maintain their social order.

One other theme has been implicit throughout the foregoing pages: man is one, but cultures vary. If this is so, then modern man is one with the primitive, and any theory of his behavior must take into account our own society along with that of the Andaman Islanders and the Australians. If we are to do this, however, we must do it with the realization that our culture is operating in the framework of evolution and the social imperatives; further, that our institutions are instrumentalities for the preservation of a people and a nation.

An examination of the formulation of the American system of government impresses one with the sociological sense that entered into the documents, creating a system of governance sufficiently rigid to provide a frame of action, yet flexible enough to meet the exigencies that prevailed during a period of unprecedented growth and change. Some of the insights show profound understanding of social forces: the dangers inherent in the provision of authority along with the equal dangers in anarchy, the problem inherent in providing for the general welfare combined with the need for recognition of individual freedom. The result was not a fortuitous one, for those who framed the Constitution did so in the light of history. Their careful analysis of the political systems of contemporary Europe and of antiquity guided them in forming our own institutions. Social planning is not a twentieth-century invention.

Their work was but a beginning, for the progress of technical evolution has not ended; the problems of institutional adjustment continue. Thus the problems of institutional adjustment are not always resolved by man consciously formulating plans to meet future exigencies; more often they are the more or less unanticipated consequences of specific acts designed to meet particular needs. We can illustrate this from current events.

Our first example has to do with the institutions of

higher learning. The postwar era has seen a remarkable advancement of education at all levels, but especially among the universities. Communities, states, and the Federal Government have been pouring money and concrete into the improvement of our college facilities. Major foundations have added to these riches, and a new phenomenon—the provision of educational facilities by big business—is coming into being. The press, which was recently decrying the universities as hotbeds of radicalism, seems now to be thoroughly in favor of an increased investment in our educational plant. It may, during a political campaign, build on ancient prejudices and decry the eggheads, but by and large it is supporting higher learning. This is neither a fad nor a response to prosperity and the economic need to consume. It is manifestly related to the functional needs of our society. It takes a great deal of skilled manpower to staff our modern technology, and the educational institutions are necessary to replenish and enrich this supply of skill. Emphasis may be upon the technicians, but not so much as one would expect, for the managerial talents are also requisite.

Meanwhile the same thing is happening elsewhere with great regularity, and this can hardly be explained as merely a matter of diffusion, though diffusion it is. Indonesia borrows our techniques and manpower to provide higher learning for its own personnel; India sends students to this country by the thousands and invites our scholars to further their training in India; England has extended educational opportunity ever more widely, because class differentials were depriving her of talent; and beyond the Iron Curtain, the great skyscraper that is the University of Moscow was raised to meet the technical needs of a growing industrialization.

That great Moscow skyscraper is relevant to the emerging attitude toward higher education in America. Popular

articles supporting the need for furthering our universities
and colleges, for revamping our program of general education, for improving the standing and salaries of professors,
have repeatedly rested their case upon this development
abroad. Such articles view with alarm the fact that the
Soviet Union is producing doctorates (and especially
physicists and engineers) at a faster rate than we are, for
they know that a technological society requires an army
of technicians. It has been said that our national budget
is drawn up in the Kremlin, and the point is relevant not
only to the present consideration but to the general thesis
of this book; for we have been at some pains to show that
the institutions of a society are not merely a matter of the
internal structure but are responsive to the environment,
and that that environment includes potential threats from
beyond the borders.

The international scene is a factor in shaping the institutions of each nation. (Something similar was shown
for the Indians of the Great Plains during the period when
some tribes received the gun, others horses, and their
neighbors had to adjust their methods of warfare—and
presumably other aspects of their behavior—to these new
external conditions.) To speak of education thus instrumentally and its current boom as a product of geopolitics
would seem to be a denial of the cultural background out
of which it grew. Our earlier use of this example demonstrated that we are not unmindful of the historical forces
that shape our present institutions of higher learning. We
are fully aware of an old and deep-seated tradition in
America which favors intellectual pursuits and the virtue
of knowledge. But we are also aware that there has always
been a contrary philosophy running along with it, decrying
learning as a perversion of man's purpose on earth. The
Greek revival and the Chatauqua circuit have as their
counterbalance the Know-Nothing Party and the mucker

pose; the popular image of a brain trust is counterbalanced by snide references to eggheads. Both sets of attitudes remain, but the situational demand gives potency to the one over the other. It is not just tradition and not merely the threat to our society from the growing power beyond our borders that have brought about the recent interest in education, for the very problem of operating an industrial society makes this higher learning a necessity.

A further illustration will show how tradition can be manipulated to fulfill institutional requirements. An examination of the history and practices of American patent law by Walton Hamilton demonstrates the potential flexibility of institutions. Hamilton shows that in the realm of patents, where customs go back to the very beginning of modern national organization and where these customs have been written down and specified in the law books, actual practice can range to the polar extremes. Comparing the glass-container industry with the automobile industry, Hamilton shows how the one was built on the authority and close control of patents while the other was built on the free exchange of such rights, so that two sets of highly self-conscious institutional practices operate within one closed cultural system. Furthermore, he shows, through an analysis of the historical development and economic circumstances of each industry, why and how these patterns came into being. The glass industry would be chaotic without control of patents, for the manufacturer of glass containers requires little specialized skill and generally available resources. It was through the control of patents that organization was provided to an otherwise amorphous and uncontrollable economic and social situation. The automobile industry also started out with an effort to maintain carefully controlled patent rights—the famed Selden patents. Very quickly, however, there developed a free licensing of patents and to this day the use of this law has little to do with divergent advantages of one automobile company over another. In the automobile industry, organization could more easily and effectively be maintained through the control of scarce material, technical skill, and developed organization, whereas the limitation on patents would only hamper expansion. The important point is that cultural background is amenable to the forces of institutional requirements, requirements which must be met if an organization is to flourish, whether it be an industry or a nation.

In our view, man is no more guided in his actions by "the dead hand of custom" than by the hand of God. The dead hand of custom is a faulty figure of speech, no longer heard in anthropological circles. Man is guided by the hand of custom, but the hand is not dead. It is rather a living, changing, and growing thing. Its viability is less easy to demonstrate from societies lacking historic records, but there is sufficient evidence to indicate its existence on the primitive as well as the civilized levels. We have already suggested the existence of such institutional adjustments on the Great Plains, and we could find examples in a variety of places.

A nice example of cultural processes that relate to the maintenance of the social order is found among the Tiv of central Nigeria. Paul Bohannan points out that in Tiv history over the past fifty years or so there have been a number of social movements which might be called anti-witchcraft. According to Bohannan these movements have taken place as a counterbalance against the concentration of power—a concentration made possible through the use of witchcraft. They are thus more or less conscious corrective movements, each one separate but all sharing the same basic pattern, serving to maintain the orderly processes of Tiv society.

Let us turn to another example from our own times to

further the matter of institutional adjustment. We are nearing the centenary of the Civil War, but the years since 1943 have seen more advancement in the position of Negroes in America than did the preceding seventy. The Congress of the United States has drawn up civil legislation of a kind not written since Reconstruction days, and the Supreme Court rulings on desegregation in the years 1954–1958 have revolutionized the legal basis for race relations in this country. Such changes can hardly be accounted for by any renewed vigor of morality, in as much as in days of prosperity man traditionally lays aside moral virtue and turns to the satisfaction of his appetites. These changes can hardly be accounted for by the influence of anthropology and sociology, which have given far less consideration to such problems in the postwar years than they did during the depression years and earlier. To some extent they may be viewed as a process of accumulated influence of earlier action, and we do not belittle the service of scholarly knowledge or the actions of moralists. Yet to see merely inertia as the force bringing about these changes is to deny the validity of another figure of speech—the swing of the pendulum.

There is actually little doubt that a major impetus for improving the condition of the Negro and for slackening discriminatory practices is a conscious reaction to pressures from abroad. The growing influence of colored groups in Asia and Africa and their role in the geopolitics of the future are not remote contingencies to the policy makers; they are the real and ever-present concerns of those who must take action. If an anthropologist among a primitive tribe on the slopes of Mt. Elgon in Uganda can feel the repercussions of a Supreme Court desegregation act, what would a journalist at Bandung, an ambassador at New Delhi, or a representative to the United Nations feel? In the context of international relations, the continuation of age-old, deeply-rooted cultural practices are dysfunctional, just as anti-Semitism was dysfunctional to Nazi Germany. American institutions are being forced to change to meet new conditions. The scholars and the moralists may rationalize the new patterns as well as provide the impetus for their development, but the institutions must change to meet the exigencies to which they are subject or the society will not long endure. It is the recognition of these needs and the appropriate action to implement them which establishes the reality of "far-sighted leadership"—and that is a judgment which can be rendered only by the historian.

The institutions of modern America, like those of all peoples everywhere, are a product of the past, having their sources deep in history. They are subject to forces that change them to fit new situations, both internally and externally. But these forces are not merely forces for change. They tend to direct the character of the transformation, to set the pattern and the style of the transformed society. Whether or not the transformation is viable depends upon the accurate calculations of those who minister to the changes and upon the flexibility of the society to make the adjustments.

Such circumstances and such actions have produced the evolutionary development of the human condition, raising man to ever greater control of his environment, to ever larger aggregates of population, to ever more complex social systems. They have taken place unrecorded and unsung in earlier eras; they continue to take place. For modern society is not the end product of such evolutionary development; it is merely at some stage along man's way.

Notes

ACKNOWLEDGMENTS

A work of synthesis such as the present essay is the product of many influences, some direct, but many obscure and indirect. These notes cannot provide a full record of such influences, but reference the more specific illustrations in the text and indicate broader sources of discussion of many major points.

I wish here to acknowledge my indebtedness to my teachers, to my colleagues, and particularly to dozens of graduate and hundreds of undergraduate students, whose questionings and proddings have helped me more than they have realized—none of whom bear responsibility for the uses to which I have put their teachings. I hesitate to mention any by name, for fear of slighting others, but assure all of my true appreciation.

CHAPTER I. THE BIOLOGICAL CONSTANT

Animal Ends and Cultural Means. Little synthetic work on the human animal is available in anthropology. A provocative statement on man is found in Earl W. Count, "The Biological Basis of Human Sociality," *Amer. Anthrop.*, Vol. 60, December, 1958. It has an extensive bibliography. On the symbol, see Leslie A. White, "The Symbol: the Origin and Basis of Human Behavior," *The Science of Culture: A Study of Man and Civilization* (Farrar, Straus, New York, 1949); also Ernst Cassirer, *An Essay on Man* (Yale University Press, New Haven, 1944); Susanne K. Langer, *Philosophy in a New Key* (Harvard University Press, Cambridge, 1942), Chapters 2 and 3; and Benjamin Lee Whorf, *Language, Thought, and Reality*, edited by John B. Carroll (Technology Press of Massachusetts Institute of Technology, Cambridge, 1956).

The Need for Positive Affect. This concept is supported by inadequate experimental data, but see: René A. Spitz, "Hospitalism: An Inquiry into the Genesis of Psychiatric Conditions in Early Childhood," *The Psychoanalytic Study of the Child*, Vol. I (International Universities Press, New York, 1945); John Bowlby, *Maternal Care and Mental Health* (World Health Organization, Geneva, 1951); and the recent studies on macaque monkeys and their response to the tactile aspect of mother surrogates as reported by Harry F. Harlow, "The Nature of Love," *American Psychologist*, Vol. 13, December, 1958. Ralph Linton expresses the same idea as "the need for emotional response" in *The Cultural Background of Personality* (Appleton-Century, New York and London, 1945), pp. 7 ff.

CHAPTER II. THE DIMENSIONS OF ANTHROPOLOGICAL THEORY

General Considerations. Anthropology is remarkably devoid of self-studies. The only histories are: the slim and dry *History of Anthropology* by Alfred C. Haddon (Watts, London, 1934); T. K. Penniman, *A Hundred Years of Anthropology*, rev. ed. (Macmillan, New York, 1952; 1st ed., 1935); and Robert H. Lowie, *The History of Ethnological Theory* (Farrar & Rinehart, New York, 1937). A recent popularized account is H. R. Hays, *From Ape to Angel* (Knopf, New York, 1958).

Classic Evolutionism. See especially: Lewis Henry Morgan, *Ancient Society* (Holt, New York, 1877); for discussion of the evolution of the family, J. J. Bachofen, *Das Mutterrecht* (Krais & Hoffman, Stuttgart, 1861); for the first study of kinship systems, Lewis H. Morgan, *Systems of Consanguinity and Affinity of the Human Family*, Smithsonian Contributions to Knowledge, Vol. 17 (Smithsonian Institution, Publication 218, Washington, D.C., 1868); Henry Maine, *Ancient Law* (Murray, London, 1861); and Edward B. Tylor, *Primitive Culture* (Murray, London, 1871). These are but a sample of a voluminous literature.

Historical Explanations. Of Franz Boas' massive products, see particularly *The Mind of Primitive Man*, rev. ed. (Macmillan, New York, 1938; 1st ed., 1911) and *Race, Language and Culture* (Macmillan, New York, 1940). On the effort to kill evolutionary theory, see in particular Robert H. Lowie, *Primitive Society* (Boni & Liveright, New York, 1920). It was in the last paragraph of this work that Lowie referred to civilization as "a thing of shreds and patches," and in the Introduction to the 1947 reprinting (Liveright) he disavowed the implication his critics gave to the phrase. Some distributional studies are: A. I. Hallowell, "Bear Ceremonialism in the Northern Hemisphere," *Amer. Anthrop.*, Vol. 28, January, 1926; Leslie Spier, *The Sun Dance of the Plains Indians: Its Development and Diffusion*, Anthropological Papers of the American Museum of Natural History, Vol. 16, Part 7 (New York, 1921); and Gudmund Hatt, *Moccasins and Their Relation to Arctic Footwear*, Memoirs of the Amer. Anthrop. Assoc., Vol. 3, No. 3 (1916). Sapir's analysis of the historical methods, "Time Perspective in Aboriginal American Culture: A Study in Method," has been republished in *Selected Writings of Edward Sapir in Language, Culture and Personality*, edited by David G. Mandelbaum (University of California Press, Berkeley, 1949); it was first published in Canada in 1916. Clark Wissler's analysis of culture history through distribution is found in *The Relation of Nature to Man in Aboriginal America* (Oxford University Press, New York and London, 1926). G. Elliot Smith, *The Ancient Egyptians and the Origin of Civilization*, rev. ed. (Harper, London and New York, 1923) and, more popularly, W. J. Perry, *The Children of the Sun* (Methuen, London, 1923) express the British view of culture emanating from Egypt. Kulturkreislehre is best seen in Wilhelm Schmidt, *Der*

Ursprung der Gottesidee, 12 vols. (Aschendorff, Münster, 1912–1955) and in F. Graebner, *Methode der Ethnologie* (Winter, Heidelberg, 1911). An evaluation was made of the point of view by Clyde Kluckhohn, "Some Reflections on the Method and Theory of the Kulturkreislehre," *Amer. Anthrop.,* Vol. 38, April, 1936. The school had wide influence in continental Europe, but the point of view is now almost abandoned.

The Sociological Orientation. The intellectual source of the sociological school was Emile Durkheim and a group of closely associated scholars (particularly Marcel Mauss) and *L'Année Sociologique,* which they published from 1898 till the First World War. English translations are now available for a number of these works: Durkheim, *The Elementary Forms of the Religious Life,* translated by J. W. Swain (Allen & Unwin, London, 1915; Macmillan, New York, 1915); Durkheim, *The Rules of Sociological Method,* translated by Sarah A. Solovay and John H. Mueller, edited by George E. G. Catlin, 8th ed. (University of Chicago Press, Chicago, 1938); Durkheim, *Suicide,* translated by John A. Spaulding and George Simpson, edited by George Simpson (Free Press, Glencoe, Ill., 1951); and Mauss, *The Gift: Forms and Functions of Exchange in Archaic Societies,* translated by Ian Cunnison (Free Press, Glencoe, Ill., 1954).

The sociological point of view has also been influenced by Max Weber —see, for example, S. F. Nadel, *Foundations of Social Anthropology* (Free Press, Glencoe, Ill., 1951)—though it seems to have been more of a back-influence, that is, a subsequent discovery of an earlier scholar with a similar outlook. A. R. Radcliffe-Brown endeavored a sociological analysis of kinship systems (contra Morgan's evolutionistic analysis) in Australia—"The Social Organization of Australian Tribes," "Oceania" Monographs, No. 1 (Macmillan, Melbourne, 1931)—and studied the Negrito people of the Andaman Islands—*The Andaman Islanders,* 2nd ed. (Cambridge University Press, Cambridge, England, 1933; Free Press, Glencoe, Ill., 1948). Radcliffe-Brown's analysis of the function of Andamanese ritual is found in Chapter 5. A number of his major essays have been reprinted in *Structure and Function in Primitive Society* (Free Press, Glencoe, Ill., 1952). The notion of clan as a corporate group was expressed by Radcliffe-Brown in his Introduction to *African Systems of Kinship and Marriage,* edited by Radcliffe-Brown and Daryll Forde (International African Institute, Oxford University Press, London, 1950). For a recent evaluation of Bronislaw Malinowski, see *Man and Culture,* edited by Raymond Firth (Routledge & K. Paul, London, 1957). His works on the Trobriand Islands include: *Argonauts of the Western Pacific* (Dutton, New York, 1950; first published, 1922); *Coral Gardens and Their Magic,* 2 vols. (American Book, New York and Chicago, 1935); *Crime and Custom in Savage Society* (K. Paul, Trench, Truebner, London, 1926; Harcourt, Brace, New York, 1926); *The Sexual Life of Savages in North-Western Melanesia* (Liveright, New York, 1929; Routledge, London, 1929).

Ruth Benedict, *Patterns of Culture* (New American Library, New York, 1946; originally Houghton, Mifflin, Boston and New York, 1934) . For related discussions of themes, see Morris Edward Opler, "Themes as Dynamic Forces in Culture," *Amer. Jour. of Sociol.,* Vol. 51, November, 1945; "Some Recently Developed Concepts Relating to Culture," *Southwestern Journal of Anthropology,* Vol. 4, Summer, 1948.

Psychological Explanations. Lucien Lévy-Bruhl, *Primitive Mentality*, translated by Lilian A. Clare (Allen & Unwin, London, 1923; Macmillan, New York, 1923), and other works. Paul Radin, *Crashing Thunder: The Autobiography of an American Indian* (Appleton, New York and London, 1926). Sigmund Freud, *Totem and Taboo*, translated by James Strachey (Routledge and K. Paul, London, 1950; Norton, New York, 1952; first published in Germany, 1912–1913). For the influence of Sapir see the section "The Interplay of Culture and Personality," in *Selected Writings of Edward Sapir in Language, Culture and Personality*, already cited. Margaret Mead's interests and publications are so widely known, starting with her *Coming of Age in Samoa* (Morrow, New York, 1928), based on a field study of the adolescent girl made in 1925–1926, that one hardly needs to set them forth. She gives a kind of autobiographical-bibliographical account in her *Male and Female: A Study of the Sexes in a Changing World* (Morrow, New York, 1949). Inexpensive, New American Library reprints of her work include *Coming of Age in Samoa, Sex and Temperament in Three Primitive Societies*, and *Growing Up in New Guinea*.

Abram Kardiner collaborated with Ralph Linton and others on *The Psychological Frontiers of Society* (Columbia University Press, New York, 1945) and with Linton on *The Individual and His Society* (Columbia University Press, New York, 1940). Linton separately published *The Cultural Background of Personality*, already cited. John J. Honigmann has published a textbook in this area, *Culture and Personality* (Harper, New York, 1954). Erik Homburger Erikson discusses the Yurok in the following: *Observations on the Yurok: Childhood and World Image*, Univ. of Calif. Pub. in Amer. Arch. and Ethnol., Vol. 35, No. 10 (Berkeley, 1943); "Childhood and Tradition in Two American Indian Tribes," *The Psychoanalytic Study of the Child*, Vol. 1 (International Universities Press, New York, 1945); and *Childhood and Society* (Norton, New York, 1950), Chapter 4. For the point of view expressed in this book, see Walter Goldschmidt, "Ethics and the Structure of Society: An Ethnological Contribution to the Sociology of Knowledge," *Amer. Anthrop.*, Vol. 53, October, 1951.

Eclecticism. See the following: Julian H. Steward, "Cultural Causality and Law: A Trial Formulation of the Development of Early Civilization," *Amer. Anthrop.*, Vol. 51, January, October, 1949; George Peter Murdock, *Social Structure* (Macmillan, New York, 1949), who follows a tradition started by E. B. Tylor in his *Researches into the Early History of Mankind and the Development of Civilization* (Murray, London, 1865); Harold E. Driver and William C. Massey, *Comparative Studies of North American Indians*, Transactions of the American Philosophical Society, new series, Vol. 47, Part 2 (Philadelphia, 1957); Clyde K. Kluckhohn and Henry A. Murray, eds., *Personality in Nature, Society and Culture*, rev. ed. (Knopf, New York, 1953).

CHAPTER III. THE SOCIAL IMPERATIVES

General Character of Social Organization. The only statement suggesting a similar point of view is in D. F. Aberle, A. K. Cohen, A. K. Davis, M. L. Levy, Jr., and F. K. Sutton, "The Functional Prerequisites of a Society,"

Ethics, Vol. 60, January, 1950. A general discussion of many of the attributes from an anthropological point of view is found in Ralph Linton, *The Study of Man* (Appleton-Century, New York, 1936) and in S. F. Nadel's *Foundations of Social Anthropology*, already cited, and his subsequent *The Theory of Social Structure* (Cohen & West, London, 1957). Modern sociological statements include Talcott Parsons and Edward A. Shils, eds., *Toward a General Theory of Action* (Harvard University Press, Cambridge, 1951), and Marion J. Levy, Jr., *The Structure of Society* (Princeton University Press, Princeton, N. J., 1952).

Groups. See: George Caspar Homans, *The Human Group* (Harcourt, Brace, New York, 1950); William F. Whyte, *Street Corner Society* (University of Chicago Press, Chicago, 1943). Walter Van Tilburg Clark, *The Ox-Bow Incident* (Random House, New York, 1940).

Values. For the Greek use of the term "areté," see Werner Jaeger, *Paideia: The Ideals of Greek Culture*, translated by Gilbert Highet, 3 vols. (Oxford University Press, New York, 1939–1944). Walter Goldschmidt, "Values and the Field of Comparative Sociology," *American Sociological Review*, Vol. 18, June, 1953. The concept of values has been subject to a great deal of discussion in anthropological circles, but its meaning is not always the same. For other treatments, see Alfred L. Kroeber, "Values as a Subject of Natural Science Inquiry," *The Nature of Culture* (University of Chicago Press, Chicago, 1952), and Clyde Kluckhohn, "Values and Value-Orientations in the Theory of Action," in Parsons and Shils, eds., *Toward a General Theory of Action*, Part 4, Chapter 2, cited above. An empirical study of values has been attempted by the philosopher Charles William Morris in *Varieties of Human Value* (University of Chicago Press, Chicago, 1956). For Plains Indian values, see, for example, Robert H. Lowie, *The Crow Indians* (Rinehart, New York, 1935 and 1956). Henri Pirenne, *Medieval Cities: Their Origins and the Revival of Trade*, translated by Frank D. Halsey (Princeton University Press, Princeton, N. J., 1925; the quotation appears on page 122 of the Doubleday Anchor Books edition (New York, 1956). Hupa religious value symbols are discussed in Walter R. Goldschmidt and Harold E. Driver, *The Hupa White Deerskin Dance*, Univ. of Calif. Pub. in Amer. Arch. and Ethnol., Vol. 35, No. 8 (Berkeley, 1940); changes in Blackfoot society in Esther S. Goldfrank, *Changing Configurations in the Social Organization of a Blackfoot Tribe During the Reserve Period*, Monographs of the American Ethnological Society, Vol. 8 (New York, 1945).

Status and Role. The best general anthropological discussion is in Linton's *The Study of Man*, already cited. The sociological literature is voluminous. For Trobriand paternal role see Bronislaw Malinowski, *Sex and Repression in Savage Society* (Routledge & K. Paul, London, 1927). On the Arunta, see Baldwin Spencer and F. J. Gillen, *The Native Tribes of Central Australia* (Macmillan, London, 1899), Chapter II. Alexis de Tocqueville, *Democracy in America*, translated by Henry Reeve (Saunders and Otley, London, 1835). Social mobility in Indian castes has been discussed in several recent studies, for example in the essays by M. N. Srinivas, Bernard S. Cohen, and Alan R. Beals in *Village India: Studies in the Little Community*, edited by McKim Marriott, Memoirs of the Amer. Anthrop. Assoc., No. 83 (1955). Edwin W. Smith and A. M. Dale, *The*

Ila-Speaking Peoples of Northern Rhodesia, 2 vols. (Macmillan, London, 1920).

Authority. There is little general discussion of authority systems in anthropological literature since Henry Maine's *Ancient Law,* already cited, but an increasing literature on primitive law: E. Adamson Hoebel, *The Law of Primitive Man: A Study in Comparative Legal Dynamics* (Harvard University Press, Cambridge, 1954). The Andamanese example is from page 45 of A. R. Radcliffe-Brown, *The Andaman Islanders;* the Ba Ila from Smith and Dale, *The Ila-Speaking Peoples of Northern Rhodesia,* cited above; the Eskimo song dueling is described, for example, in Knud Rasmussen, *Across Arctic America* (Putnam, New York, 1927). For Yurok see especially A. L. Kroeber, "Law of the Yurok Indians," *Atti del XXII Congresso Internazionale degli Americanisti,* Vol. 2, 1926 (Rome, 1928); for Ifugao, see R. F. Barton, *Ifugao Law,* Univ. of Calif. Pub. in Amer. Arch. and Ethnol., Vol. 15, No. 1 (Berkeley, 1919). The Eskimo-Shoshone similarity is pointed up by Ralph L. Beals and Harry Hoijer, *An Introduction to Anthropology* (Macmillan, New York, 1953), pp. 446 ff. On Highlands New Guinea, see, for instance, Abraham L. Gitlow, *Economics of the Mount Hagan Tribes, New Guinea,* Monographs of the American Ethnological Society, Vol. 12 (New York, 1947); for secret societies, see Hutton Webster, *Primitive Secret Societies,* 2nd, rev. ed. (Macmillan, New York, 1932), and Robert H. Lowie, *Plains Indian Age-Societies,* Anthropological Papers of the American Museum of Natural History, Vol. 11, Part 13 (New York, 1916). For Weber's discussion of bureaucracy, see "Bureaucracy," in *From Max Weber: Essays in Sociology,* translated and edited by H. H. Gerth and C. Wright Mills (Oxford University Press, New York, 1946), originally from *Wirtschaft und Gesellschaft.* The discussion of the Baganda is based upon Rev. John Roscoe, *The Baganda: An Account of Their Native Customs and Beliefs* (Macmillan, London, 1911).

Ideology. Tlingit law is from Kalervo Oberg, "Crime and Punishment in Tlingit Society," *Amer. Anthrop.,* Vol. 36, April, 1934; also see his Ph.D. dissertation, *The Social Economy of the Tlingit Indians* (University of Chicago, 1940). For general description of Tlingit, see Aurel Krause, *The Tlingit Indians,* translated by Erna Gunther (American Ethnological Society, 1956), originally published as *Die Tlinkit-Indianer,* in Jena, 1885. Robert K. Merton, "The Self-Fulfilling Prophecy," *The Antioch Review,* Vol. 8, Summer, 1948.

CHAPTER IV. THE MECHANISMS OF SOCIAL EVOLUTION

Though there is a broad and continuing literature on social evolution, I know of no place where the mechanisms by which such evolution takes place are discussed. The line of argument presented here is implicit in Walter Goldschmidt, "Social Organization in Native California and the Origin of Clans," *Amer. Anthrop.,* Vol. 50, July, 1948. Leslie A. White shows that evolutionary development rests upon the harnessing of energy: "Energy and the Evolution of Culture," *The Science of Culture: A Study of Man and Civilization* (Farrar, Straus, New York, 1949). George Orwell, *Animal Farm* (Harcourt, Brace, New York, 1946). For the Siriono, see

Allan R. Holmberg, *Nomads of the Long Bow: The Siriono of Eastern Bolivia* (Institute of Social Anthropology, Smithsonian Institution, No. 10, Washington, D. C., 1950).

The Evolution of Technology. See the encyclopedic study *A History of Technology*, edited by Charles Singer, E. J. Holmyard, and A. R. Hall, 5 vols. (Oxford University Press, New York, 1954–1957). For ecological analysis, see Julian H. Steward, *Basin-Plateau Aboriginal Sociopolitical Groups* (Bureau of American Ethnology, Bulletin 120, Washington, 1938).

The Selective Process in Evolution. S. F. Nadel, "Witchcraft in Four African Societies," *Amer. Anthrop.*, Vol. 54, January, 1952. A. R. Radcliffe-Brown, *The Andaman Islanders;* Walter Goldschmidt, "Ethics and the Structure of Society"—both already cited. See the story "Wolf Lies Down" in K. N. Llewellyn and E. Adamson Hoebel, *The Cheyenne Way: Conflict and Case Law in Primitive Jurisprudence* (University of Oklahoma Press, Norman, 1941), pp. 127 ff. Leopold Poposil, "Social Change and Primitive Law: Consequences of a Papuan Legal Case," *Amer. Anthrop.*, Vol. 60, October, 1958. Mischa Titiev, *Old Oraibi: A Study of the Hopi Indians of Third Mesa*, Papers of the Peabody Museum of American Archaeology and Ethnology, Vol. 22, No. 1 (Harvard University, Cambridge, 1944). Robert H. Lowie, *The Crow Indians*, Chapter II, already cited. Alexander Spoehr, *Changing Kinship Systems*, Field Museum of Natural History, Anthropological Series, Vol. 33, No. 4 (Chicago, 1947). Edward P. Dozier, *The Changing Social Organization of the Hopi-Tewa*, Ph.D. dissertation (Univ. of Calif., Los Angeles, 1954), Chap. IV. For Araucanian kinship, see Mischa Titiev, *Araucanian Culture in Transition*, Occasional Contributions from the Museum of the University of Michigan, No. 15 (Ann Arbor, 1951), and Louis C. Faron, "Araucanian Patri-Organization and the Omaha System," *Amer. Anthrop.*, Vol. 58, June, 1956. Henri Pirenne, *Medieval Cities*, already cited. For the Aztecs, see George C. Vaillant, *Aztecs of Mexico* (Doubleday, Garden City, N. Y., 1941). For Baganda occupational clans: Roscoe's *The Baganda*, already cited. Walton Hale Hamilton, *Patents and Free Enterprise* (Temporary National Economic Committee, Monograph No. 31, Senate Committee Print, 76th Congress, 3rd Session, Washington, D.C., 1941). For Incas, see P. A. Means, *Ancient Civilizations of the Andes* (Scribner, New York, 1931). For Plains history, Frank Raymond Secoy, *Changing Military Patterns on the Great Plains*, Monographs of the American Ethnological Society, Vol. 21 (New York, 1953).

Continuity in Social Evolution. Walter Goldschmidt, "Social Organization in Native California and the Origin of Clans," already cited. James West, *Plainville, U.S.A.* (Columbia University Press, New York, 1945). Raymond Firth, *Primitive Economics of the New Zealand Maori* (Dutton, New York, 1929). For a short discussion of the alphabet, see A. L. Kroeber, "The Story of the Alphabet," in *Anthropology*, rev. ed. (Harcourt, Brace, New York, 1948). Elton Mayo, *The Human Problems of an Industrial Civilization* (Macmillan, New York, 1933). Ruth Benedict, *Patterns of Culture*, and M. E. Opler, "Themes as Dynamic Forces in Culture"—already cited. Esther Goldfrank, *Changing Configurations in the Social Organization of a Blackfoot Tribe During the Reserve Period*, already cited.

Congruity in Social Patterning. Ruth Benedict, *Patterns of Culture,* and M. E. Opler, "Themes as Dynamic Forces in Culture," both already cited. R. H. Tawney, *Religion and the Rise of Capitalism* (Murray, London, 1926; Harcourt, Brace, New York, 1926). Max Weber, *The Protestant Ethic and the Spirit of Capitalism,* translated by Talcott Parsons (Allen and Unwin, London, 1930). Elton Mayo, *The Human Problems of an Industrial Civilization* (Macmillan, New York, 1933).

CHAPTER V. EVOLUTION AND THE SOCIAL IMPERATIVES

The Evolution of Technology. V. Gordon Childe, *What Happened in History* (Penguin Books, New York, 1946); and *Man Makes Himself* (Oxford University Press, New York, 1939). Joseph R. Caldwell, *Trend and Tradition in the Prehistory of the Eastern United States,* Memoirs of the Amer. Anthrop. Assoc. No. 88 (1958).

Evolutionary Change in Groups. For patrilineal tendency in hunting-gathering bands, see George P. Murdock, "World Ethnographic Sample," *Amer. Anthrop.,* Vol. 59, August, 1957. A. R. Radcliffe-Brown, *The Andaman Islanders;* Walter Goldschmidt, "Social Organization in Native California and the Origin of Clans"; John Roscoe, *The Baganda;* George C. Vaillant, *Aztecs of Mexico*—all already cited. Martin C. Yang, *A Chinese Village: Taitou, Shantung Province* (Columbia University Press, New York, 1945), pp. 134 ff; Francis Hsü, *Under the Ancestors' Shadow* (Columbia University Press, New York, 1948), pp. 122 ff. Sir Baldwin Spencer and F. J. Gillen, *The Arunta: A Study of a Stone Age People,* 2 vols. (Macmillan, London, 1927).

Evolutionary Change in Values. Thomas R. Garth, Jr., "Emphasis on Industriousness Among the Atsugewi," *Amer. Anthrop.,* Vol. 47, October, 1945. Bronislaw Malinowski, *Coral Gardens and Their Magic,* Vol. 1, already cited. Hester's statement appears in Sylvanus Griswold Morley, *The Ancient Maya,* 3rd ed., revised by George W. Brainerd (Stanford University Press, Stanford, Calif., 1957), Notes to Chap. VIII, pp. 453 ff. Charles Hose and W. McDougall, *The Pagan Tribes of Borneo,* 2 vols. (Macmillan, London, 1912). Audrey I. Richards, *Land, Labour and Diet in Northern Rhodesia* (Oxford University Press, London, 1939). Emile Durkheim, *Suicide,* already cited. Edward Sapir, "Culture, Genuine and Spurious," in *Selected Writings,* already cited; this essay was first published in *Amer. Jour. of Sociol.,* Vol. 29, January, 1924.

The Evolution of Status. Cora Du Bois, *The People of Alor* (University of Minnesota Press, Minneapolis, 1944). Mary Antoinette Czaplicka, *The Evolution of the Cossack Communities* (Billing and Sons, Guildford, 1918).

The Evolution of Social Roles. A. R. Radcliffe-Brown, *The Andaman Islanders,* and Spencer and Gillen, *The Arunta,* pp. 443 ff.—both already cited. Karl A. Wittfogel, *Oriental Despotism: A Comparative Study of Total Power* (Yale University Press, New Haven, 1957). Roscoe, *The Baganda,* Chapters 7 and 8. Kofi Abrefa Busia, *The Position of the Chief in the Modern Political System of Ashanti* (Oxford University Press, London, 1951). Smith and Dale, *The Ila-Speaking Peoples of Northern Rhodesia,* already cited.

Ideological Development. A. van Gennep, *Les Rites de Passage* (Nourry, Paris, 1909). Max Weber, *The Protestant Ethic and the Spirit of Capitalism,* and R. H. Tawney, *Religion and the Rise of Capitalism*—both already cited.

CHAPTER VI. THE EVOLUTION OF SOCIETY

Nomadic Hunting and Food-Gathering Societies. Allan Holmberg, *Nomads of the Long Bow,* cited earlier.

Sedentary Hunting and Food-Gathering Societies. A. L. Kroeber, *Cultural and Natural Areas of Native and North America,* Univ. of Calif. Pub. in Amer. Arch. and Ethnol., Vol. 38 (Berkeley, 1939). V. G. Childe, *What Happened in History,* pp. 34 ff. Alfred L. Kroeber, *Handbook of the Indians of California* (Bureau of American Ethnology, Smithsonian Institution, Bulletin 78, Washington, D. C., 1925). For Yurok property, see T. T. Waterman, *Yurok Geography,* Univ. of Calif. Pub. in Amer. Arch. and Ethnol., Vol. 16, No. 5 (Berkeley, 1920); for Tlingit property, see Viola Garfield, "Historical Aspects of Tlingit Clans in Angoon, Alaska," *Amer. Anthrop.,* Vol. 49, July, 1947; Walter Goldschmidt and Theodore H. Haas, *Possessory Rights of the Natives of Southeastern Alaska,* mimeographed (Office of Indian Affairs, U.S. Department of Interior, October, 1946). A. H. Gayton, *Yokuts-Mono Chiefs and Shamans,* Univ. of Calif. Pub. in Amer. Arch. and Ethnol., Vol. 24, No. 8 (Berkeley, 1930).

Agricultural Societies. The best short statements of urbanization theory are by Louis Wirth: "The Urban Society and Civilization," *Eleven Twenty-Six: A Decade of Social Science Research,* edited by Louis Wirth (University of Chicago Press, Chicago, 1940), and his "Urbanism as a Way of Life," *Amer. Jour. of Sociol.,* Vol. 42, 1938. For the classic treatment, see Ferdinand Tönnies, *Gemeinschaft und Gesellschaft* (Leipzig, 1887), translated and edited by Charles P. Loomis under the title *Fundamental Concepts of Sociology* (American Book, New York, 1940). For African development, see Kenneth Little, "The Role of Voluntary Associations in West African Urbanization," *Amer. Anthrop.,* Vol. 59, August, 1957, and his *The Mende of Sierra Leone: A West African People in Transition* (Routledge & K. Paul, London, 1951). For folk societies, see Robert Redfield, "The Folk Society," *Amer. Jour. of Sociol.,* Vol. 52, January, 1947, and his recent *The Little Community* (University of Chicago Press, Chicago, 1955). George M. Foster, "What Is Folk Culture?" *Amer. Anthrop.,* Vol. 55, April-June, 1953. James West, *Plainville, U.S.A.,* and Francis Hsü, *Under the Ancestors' Shadow*—both cited earlier. Fustel de Coulanges, *The Ancient City,* translated by Willard Small (Doubleday Anchor Books, Garden City, N. Y., 1956), first published as *La Cité Antique* (1864).

Herding Societies. Elizabeth E. Bacon, *Obok: A Study of Social Structure,* Viking Fund Publications in Anthropology, No. 25, 1958. Walter Prescott Webb, *The Great Plains* (Ginn, Boston, 1931). Frank Raymond Secoy, *Changing Military Patterns on the Great Plains,* and Esther Goldfrank, *Changing Configurations in the Social Organization of a Blackfoot Tribe During the Reserve Period*—both already cited.

Industrial Societies. Walter Goldschmidt, *As You Sow* (Harcourt, Brace,

New York, 1947); also *Small Business and the Community* (Senate, Committee Print No. 13, 79th Congress, 2nd Session, Washington, D. C., 1946).

CHAPTER VII. THE SCIENTIFIC STUDY OF SOCIETY

Paul Radin, *Primitive Man as Philosopher* (Appleton, New York and London, 1927). Melville J. Herskovits, *The Economic Life of Primitive Peoples* (Knopf, New York, 1940); the second, revised edition was entitled *Economic Anthropology: A Study in Comparative Economics* (Knopf, New York, 1952). Paul Bohannan, "Extra-Processual Events in Tiv Political Institutions," *Amer. Anthrop.*, Vol. 60, February, 1958. Llewellyn and Hoebel, *The Cheyenne Way*, already cited. Walton Hamilton, *Patents and Free Enterprise*, already cited. John Adair and Evon Vogt, "Navaho and Zuni Veterans: A Study of Contrasting Modes of Culture Change," *Amer. Anthrop.*, Vol. 51, October, 1949.

Index

247

ABOUT THE AUTHOR

Walter Goldschmidt is Professor of Anthropology and Sociology at the University of California, Los Angeles. He was born in San Antonio, Texas, and graduated from the University of Texas at the age of twenty. He received his doctorate in Anthropology from the University of California, Berkeley, made several studies of the social behavior of California Indians, and then turned his attention to anthropological studies of modern California communities. He has also made field trips to Alaska for the Office of Indian Affairs and to Uganda under a Fulbright grant. After studying the Sebei tribe he drove five thousand miles through Africa.

Dr. Goldschmidt has always been interested in making the subject matter of his science accessible to a wide audience, as well as preparing technical papers for his colleagues. Of the present volume, *Man's Way,* he writes, "I think it is possible to phrase our scientific understandings so that they are clear to any intelligent reader; I suspect obscure writing always masks obscure thinking." His interest in popular presentation started as a graduate student in Berkeley, when he assisted the late Miguel Covarrubias in preparing his famous map murals of the Pacific area. From 1951 to 1953 he was the Director of the Ways of Mankind radio project—a series of broadcasts designed to communicate the ideas of anthropology to a popular audience; selections of these scripts were later published under the titles *Ways of Mankind* and

About the Author

Ways to Justice. Among his other books have been *As You Sow* and *The United States and Africa* (of which he was the editor).

In 1956 Dr. Goldschmidt was appointed Editor of the *American Anthropologist*, the official organ of the American Anthropological Association.

He lives in Los Angeles with his wife and two sons.